stanisic LIVE/WORK

Pesaro Publishing

First published in 2011 by Pesaro Publishing

Editor: Patrick Bingham-Hall
Design: Pesaro Publishing and Ayeemm Cabales

Text © Anna Johnson, Philip Drew, Tom Henaghan, Tarsha Finney
and Pesaro Publishing

Photography © Patrick Bingham-Hall and where otherwise credited

Pesaro Publishing
PO Box 74
Balmain NSW 2041
Sydney, Australia

Pesaro Publishing
14 Robinson Road #13-00
Far East Finance Building
Singapore 048545

www.pesaropublishing.com

National Library of Australia Cataloguing-in-Publication entry

Title: Stanisic - live work : the architecture of stanisic architects - frank stanisic / editor and photographer, Patrick Bingham-Hall ; contributors, Anna Johnson, Philip Drew, Tarsha Finney and Tom Heneghan.

ISBN: 9781877015311

Subjects: Stanisic, Frank.
Stanisic Associates Architects.
Architectural firms--Australia.
Architects--Australia.
Architecture--Australia--21st century.
Architecture and society--Australia.

Other Authors/Contributors:
Bingham-Hall, Patrick.
Johnson, Anna Christine, 1971-
Finney, Tarsha.
Heneghan, Tom.
Drew, Philip.

Dewey Number: 720.994

All rights reserved. No part of this publication may be reproduced, stored in, or introduced to, a retrieval system or transmitted in any form or by any means, electronic, mechanical, photocopying, recording or otherwise, without the prior written permission of the publishers.

ISBN 978-1-877015-31-1

Printed by Imago

stanisic LIVE/WORK
2000-2010

Introductory Essay and
Project Text by Anna Johnson

Photography by Patrick Bingham-Hall

contents

6	live/work : Anna Johnson
30	domain
36	presidio
42	atlas
48	mondrian
64	spectrum
72	datum
80	222
90	coda
108	elsie
114	waterside/(form)matrix
122	zone
130	edo
146	era
162	dunning
168	prince henry
172	quay
176	mission
184	roseville
192	hyperform
60	mondrian : Philip Drew
106	coda : Tarsha Finney
142	edo : Tom Heneghan
198	acknowledgments
199	awards

opposite : Era,
Kings Cross, 2005-2009

LIVE/WORK

Anna Johnson

Anna Johnson is a lecturer in architectural design and communications at the School of Architecture and Design, RMIT University, Melbourne, where she is also Coordinator of Asian Urbanism and Architecture.

opposite page : Coda, Rosebery, 2002-2008

1 Boyd, Robin, *Australia's Home*, 2nd edition, Penguin, Melbourne, 1978, p8.

In 1952 Robin Boyd wrote, "Australia is the small house… the suburban way of life and the aspiration to own and occupy a detached house have long been Australian characteristics."[1] Nearly 60 years down the track, this sentiment remains relevant and has gained momentum as late-capitalist culture drives a population determinedly towards conspicuous consumption and the prize of the designed possession. Indeed architects today are as much in the business of providing for a society hungry for things and for the elevation of lifestyle these 'products' promise. Whilst the utopian social agendas aspired to by architects at the beginning of the 20th century were not without their failings, a desire for a consequential relationship between architects, the social issues of housing, and the formation of the city, is now only pursued by some architects, and few have sufficient power to radically alter the development of our cities.

In the early 21st century, the architecturally designed house – large and ostentatious with bathrooms aplenty – dominates architectural publication. Books and magazines praise

above: *parti* sketch of 222, Alexandria, 2002-2009

2 Brew, Peter, 'Modern Flats', in Simon Anderson and Meaghan Nordeck, *Krantz and Sheldon Architectural Projects*, University of Western Australia, Perth, 1996, p6

3 Butler-Bowden, Caroline and Pickett, Charles, *Homes in the Sky: Apartment Living in Australia*, The Miegunyah Press, Historic Houses Trust, Sydney, 2007.

and lavishly document the architectural sophistication of rarefied buildings that do not and cannot hold the answer to an environmentally or socially sustainable future. Apartments, or 'collective housing' as Frank Stanisic describes them, and the various hybrid configurations they champion, have only recently emerged from the margins, and are now becoming more widely accepted as a desirable form of accommodation. Over the last several years Stanisic's buildings have gained architectural recognition: Mondrian won the 2003 Wilkinson Award, and Edo was awarded the inaugural 2008 Aaron Bolot Award and the 2008 Frederick Romberg Award for residential buildings. This increasing acceptance of collective housing as legitimate architectural territory reflects the overseas experience where the design of collective housing in Spain, Denmark, Austria, Holland, France and Germany constitutes much architectural practice. Books such as Hilary French's *New Urban Housing* and the *a+t Density* series of publications carefully document a great diversity of collective housing and hybrid projects, and illustrate the growing interest that the profession, universities and general public have in this evolving typology.

Upon graduating from the University of Sydney in 1978, Stanisic joined the office of the well-known Australian modernist architect John Andrews and spent a year in Washington working on the design of the Intelsat Satellite Headquarters, won by the office through international competition. He followed this with a stint in Ken Woolley's office, before working for Lawrence Nield and Partners. From Andrews he gained an insight into a very conceptually driven approach to design whilst, by contrast, he was then exposed to the Woolley's 'direct' detailing and careful exploration of materiality. It was Nield, however, who was most fundamentally concerned with urbanism, and it was in his practice that Stanisic developed his abiding interest in the interface of building and street.

In 1990, Stanisic began his own practice, splitting his time between designing projects and teaching in design studios at all three Sydney architecture schools. At UTS he taught for 4 years with Peter John Cantrill, Tony Caro and Russell Olsson in a course headed by Associate Professor Winston Barnett: an iconoclast and provocateur, who ran a graduation design studio that privileged 'big picture' thinking and focused on large scale urban projects and masterplans. It gave Stanisic the opportunity to test urban propositions within an experimental teaching environment where the favoured design tactic was 'transforming the type', and to build up a storehouse of ideas that were to surface in his early projects.

Stanisic later collaborated with several of his former students and Hassell Architects to win an international competition for a 'sustainable city' at Green Square, a 275 hectare brownfield site four kilometres south of Sydney's CBD. The success of the Green Square Master Plan – and subsequent collective housing and urban renewal projects – established Stanisic as one of Sydney's leading architects in the field of sustainable apartments. The work of the practice, concerned with what Stanisic describes as "authentic and modern architecture that reflects the specific cultural values and social shifts, rather than the style of the day," asserts a design platform of 'Eco Minimalism': the exploration of space, light, sun and materiality to produce a climatically responsive modernist architecture.

The concern of Stanisic Associates is with the city, and central to this enquiry are questions of the city's sustainable growth, its life and culture, and its ability to support a dramatically increasing population. The work is driven not so much by questions of aesthetics and form, but by difficult questions of appropriate density, and by the design of sustainable typologies to provide new ways of working and living in buildings that address the city fabric and facilitate dynamic street life. Collective housing (and its hybrid variations) is one of the most difficult typologies with which to establish a critical architectural practice in a marketplace dominated by 'volume' builders and developers. This type of architecture and its architects, as practitioner and academic Peter Brew has observed, "remain outside official histories… and pose a problem… because they do not affirm the egalitarian myth of the nuclear family with the Hills Hoist and mortgage."[2]

Christine Butler-Bowden and Charles Picket's *Homes in the Sky: Apartment Living in Australia* [3] is the first comprehensive publication that documents the history of apartment buildings in Australia, but this book was authored and initiated by social and cultural theorists rather than by architects or the architectural profession. More recently, architects and academics are publishing and researching broader questions of appropriate housing, sustainability, population growth and changing demographics. The publications and work by MAS (the Monash Architecture Studio, led by Professor Shane Murray and Diego Ramirez-Lovering) demonstrate their underlying concern as to how architecture can contribute to society, the environment and housing in a substantial, far-reaching and sustainable manner. Their research addresses what they describe as the problematic relationship between architecture and housing in Australia, driven as it is by the production and marketing of highly expensive one-off houses for an elite clientele.

For the most part, the commonly held perception is that apartment (or 'flat') typology and its variants do not compete with the house as a valid form of accommodation or as a real form of architectural experimentation, yet the reality could not be further from the truth. As Butler-Bowden and Picket point out, "today more flats than houses are being built in Melbourne, Sydney and Perth... urban demographics predict that by 2030, 45 per cent of Sydney households will be living in flats,"[4] so more than ever, the production of alternative forms of living, and of the occupation of our cities is imperative. Whilst the current method of rescuing our cities has been – as Brew argues – to build houses, this has been "restricted to interpreting two paradigmatic models, that of the terrace and the villa."[5] Until recently, the Australian city has been largely studied in terms of a few particular building types, those of the house, the office, the warehouse, and the public institution, whilst apartments and mixed use – the types that concern Stanisic Associates – have been largely excluded. As Stanisic says, "If you want to read the changes in a society, then look no further than its housing design. Housing is a form of cultural design, it is as significant as the design of iconic public structures. More than any other form of architecture, housing responds quickly to cultural shifts: demographic, economic and environmental. Housing is possibly more important than the iconic buildings, as our living environment determines the way we see our world."

Beyond the environmental and social potentials of collective housing, radical architectural invention has occurred within the historical evolution of this type. As Butler-Bowden and Picket argue, apartment buildings have "formed the architectural cutting edge of social and cultural change... and provided an architectural context for the emergence of social groups distinct from the suburban mainstream." More specifically, apartments designed by architects since World War II serve – more than any other type – as a way to understand the real implications of modernist architecture in Australia beyond a series of generalisations concerning form, style and "themes of innocence, directness or optimism."[6] Experiments in apartment architecture – of planning, circulation, sectional configurations, room use and functionality, access to green space and public amenities – form many of the central components of spatially rich and inventive architecture.

The avant garde housing experiments of the early 20th century, especially in the newly formed Soviet Union and central Europe, were the essential precedents for the formation of the 'modern flat' as we now understand it, and remain primary inspirations for Stanisic Associates. Excellent examples of apartments and their variants can be found across all Australia's large cities, and Stanisic (a committed Sydneysider) has also looked to such local examples as the series of mid-century modernist apartments located throughout Potts Point and Elizabeth Bay. Aaron Bolot's Wylde Street Cooperative Apartments (1948-52), with its dramatic radially-planned expression of democratic modernism,[7] and the Ithica (1960) and Aquarius (1965) apartments by Harry Seidler are perhaps the most noteworthy. Whilst Stanisic observes that the Seidler buildings "do not activate the street", and do not perform the important civic role of creating a public realm and maintaining an active streetscape, Seidler's ruthless determination and skilful planning created well-ventilated, light-filled, efficient apartments that capture the views and the northeast sea breezes.

Stanisic Associates work in a very different context to the harbourside location of those modernist apartments, and their response to these less spectacular settings is one of the distinguishing features of their architecture. Their context is that of the industrial working class suburbs of Alexandria, Waterloo, Rosebery and Zetland – an area now known as Green Square – just south of the city of Sydney: brownfield sites that have no connection with the iconic harbourside sites of elite apartments. Characterised by an unremarkable

opposite page : 222, Alexandria, 2002-2009

4   Butler-Bowden and Picket, 2007, p5

5   Brew, Peter, 1996, p5

6   Brew, 1996, p7

7   Butler-Bowden and Picket, 2007, p109

landscape of factories and warehouses, and now colonised by a swathe of developer-driven apartments, these sites for the southern Sydney projects are tough, and require a resolute yet inventive vision. With no views, no sea breezes and very little romance, the demands upon the architect are great: to resurrect a sense of place, and to create accommodation and active public space where none have existed. Typological and architectural invention cannot rely on the 'scenographic', but must provide for one. With their more affordable land prices and a promise of high returns, these sites are very attractive for the developer-builder, which further affects the conditions in which Stanisic Associates operate. As Stanisic states, this field is "a well and truly occupied territory," a highly competitive field where architects must work economically, and offer financially viable alternatives to the developer model of mass housing. Stanisic continues, " The statutory and advisory documents offer basic guidance, but their policing by local councils is so pathetically inadequate that green initiatives can be easily undermined by an unwilling client. You are on your own in this field, in an often indifferent and predatory environment, where you sometimes need to take the law in your own hands and create your own version of the truth to get what you really want."

With their competitive housing and hybrid models – possessing environmental passive design imperatives – and planning and typological innovations, Stanisic Associates have established an unprecedented standard of design for these brownfield conditions, which places them at the vanguard of this difficult terrain. Their competitors are not so much the 'high end' architects who produce boutique apartments – such as Ian Moore, Alex Tzannes, Fender Katsalidis, Elenberg Fraser or Wood Marsh – but large property developers. Although form and aesthetics are important to Stanisic Associates, their ambitions are more concerned with questions of appropriate environmentally-responsive types and

relationships with the city. The practice is committed to the evolution of a flexible system that allows for alternative models for living and working: one that has, at its core, the desire to create passively designed architecture that responds to the city and its liveability, and the need to accommodate a swelling population. The limitations of the developers' models are well-known: the flabby outmoded planning, and poorly oriented buildings thinly veiled in period style, are described by Frank Stanisic as "a fruit salad of form, colour and detail." Although the market has been driven by the developers' model, the advantages of the approach taken by Stanisic Associates – with its ingenious planning and typological invention, with flexible well-lit and well-ventilated spaces – has become evident.

Aesthetically, the work of Stanisic Associates has seen decreasing reference to an overtly formal architectural style or idiom. The first series of iterations – projects such as Atlas, Datum, Spectrum and Mondrian – revealed an architectural language derived from the Russian avant-garde and European modernism of the early 20th century. The architectural elements of gallery and corridor, access, circulation and the variety of apartment types are clearly expressed, and the arrangement establishes a tension between the linear, robust, muscular forms, and the light, glazed elements of the access galleries and windows, with a finer layer of screens and awnings. As the practice became more concerned with refining an essential system of frame or form overlaid with an environmental skin, the form itself – driven by issues of technology and environmental responsiveness – has become more abstract and more diagrammatic. The geometric, structural and material clarity of recent projects resonates superficially with contemporary evolutions of late-style international modernism, but they are more clearly driven by the architects' idea of a framework, of a structural shell, which supports a flexible system of dwellings with protected outdoor spaces and operable environmental screens that form naturally ventilated 'unplugged environments'. We see this most clearly exemplified in EDO, which reads as a visible framework supporting a series of variable and operable 'glittering' screens.

Further themes emerge in the most recent projects, and Coda especially represents these shifts. Whilst the form – tall and slim, with its carriage following the road's natural curvature – gives this building a particular dynamic, the environmental screens have become more skin than screen, and draped over the form, the screens' operability and metallic materiality give the building a kinetic quality. This *parti* of a dynamic kinetic screen wrapped over form is dramatically expressed in Roseville and Hyperform, two unbuilt larger scale hybrid projects. With these buildings the aesthetic quality of the architecture results from the impact of the louvred skins: Roseville is lit with coloured LED lights, whilst Hyperform wraps a highly sculpted form. One of the intentions is to push the expression so that the interior program is completely ambiguous from the exterior, which by contrast establishes its own dialogue and interaction with the city and the streetscape below.

opposite page : Atlas, Alexandria, 2000-2002

Live/Work - Anna Johnson

A smaller scaled theme has surfaced in recent work, for example in Era, whereby a certain 'poetry' of expression was derived from the structure and its formal responsiveness to climate and the environment. Whilst Stanisic has been quoted as being a 'green heretic' – an architect who does not want to be characterised as a 'green architect' but rather as a 'good architect' – a certain irony exists. Whilst the buildings adapt and accommodate the social issues of changing density and demographics, the architects have developed a finally tuned response to climate and the environment. The reciprocity that exists between the environment and the architecture is not overt or signalled by formal gestures typical of green environmentally responsive architecture. Nevertheless, in projects such as Era, certain details are completely driven by their environmental context, and become a register, a quite literal expression of that particular climatic behaviour. The 'poetry' of this fusing of technology, structure, and the environment, is one the architects wish to pursue further.

A critical planning strategy that recurs across all Stanisic projects is the crossover section: an organising principle whereby the sleeping and washing areas on the upper floor cross over the entry and living areas of a two-storey compartment, thus creating a double frontage, and stimulating air-flow down the stairs and through the living space. This 'gallery crossover' section emerged from Stanisic's investigation of the 'down and under' or 'up and over' sections of the Russian Constructivists, then appropriated by Le Corbusier for his Unite d'Habitation (1946-52) in Marseille. Stanisic vertically sliced the section in half, connecting the access and circulation spaces to the exterior of the shady southern side, whilst having all living areas and balconies located on the sunny northern side. Stanisic Associates use several variations of this type across

left : Era,
Kings Cross, 2005-2009

opposite : EDO,
Woolloomooloo, 2005-2007

8 Borden, Iain, 'Skateboarding' in Malcolm Miles and Tim Hall with Iain Borden (eds), *The City Cultures Reader*, 2nd Edition, Routledge, London and New York, 2003, p292

their projects: the 'gallery crossover' is one transformation whereby the circulation is expressed on the building's exterior, whilst achieving a climatically responsive living environment with natural light entering all habitable rooms. Other variations of the standard crossover type include a double crossover, a triple crossover, a loft crossover, and a 'crossunder' with a bedroom entry level, with all possessing either enclosed, screened, or open galleries. As Stanisic says, "the 'gallery crossover' fundamentally supports one of our essential organising principles for passive housing design… live in the sun, walk in the shade."

The City and its Architecture: A Question of Typology.

Stanisic's work begins with the city: his passion is the city's life and culture, and importantly, its sustainability and liveability. But for this architect, as with many practitioners who don't conform to the dominant paradigms of urban design or architecture, he looks to other sources – vernacular urbanisms, events, and experiences more directly connected to the fabric and reality of the city – and one of his inspirations is the hip-hop and rap of street music. In his *'A Performative Critique of the City: The Urban Practice of Skateboarding, 1958-98'*, Iain Borden (Bartlett Professor of Architecture) looks to the skateboarder as an urban practitioner and, like Borden, Stanisic argues that in urban space, the life of the city comes less from canonised texts and representations than it does from those directly engaged in the imaginative experience of the city space and life. Skateboarders represent their practice through their engagement with the city, with what they do, see, and experience: their relationship with the street is what activates the experience. They "reject both the values and the spatio-temporal modes of living in the capitalist city" and instead, they seek an alternative occupation that "that runs across its terrains" and is indifferent to function or ideological content.[8] Whilst Stanisic does not operate as an urban performer or musician, he seeks a dialogue with the city that is intensely active and alive, such as EDO's restaurant interface to the street, 222's street level retail interface, or Mondrian's through-site public way.

opposite page: *parti* sketch of Mission, Haymarket, 2008-

9   Koolhaas, Rem, 'What ever happened to Urbanism?' in Rem Koolhaas and Bruce Mau, *S,M,L,XL*, 010 Publishers, New York, First Edition, 1995, p959

10 Koolhaas, Rem, 1995, p963

11 Vidler, Anthony, 'The Third Typology' in K. Michael Hays (Ed), *Architecture Theory since 1968*, The MIT Press, New York, 2000.

12 Vidler, 2000, p291

13 Vidler, 2000, p292

14 Vidler, 2000, p293

15 Ebner, Peter; Herrman, Eva; Hollbacher, Roman; Kunstcher, Markus; and Wietzorrek, Ulrike, '*Typology + Innovative Residential Architecture*', Birkhauser, Basel, 2010, p15

16 Ebner, Peter; Herrman, Eva; Hollbacher, Roman; Kunstcher, Markus; and Wietzorrek, Ulrike, 2010, p15

17 Stoppani, Teresa, 'Seven thoughts on a sin (typology)' in *Negation in Art and Architecture*, 66 East, Centre for Urban Culture, Amsterdam, 2005, pp12-13

18 Stoppani, Teresa, pp12-13

Rem Koolhaas – an urbanist whose influence on the architectural profession's conception of the city, and on the relationship between architecture and culture, is omnipresent – states emphatically that "the city no longer exists."[9] In his influential piece *What Ever Happened to Urbanism?*, Koolhaas argues that the very concept of the city has been "distorted and stretched" and that any attempt to define its "images, rules and fabrication… irrevocably leads via nostalgia to irrelevance." Architecture, he continues, "defies, excludes, limits, separates from the 'rest'… and exhausts the potentials that can be generated finally only by urbanism." Koolhaas proposes that if there is to be a new urbanism, it will not be based on "order and omnipotence, but rather on the staging of uncertainty… [it] will be about expanding notions, denying boundaries… discovering unnameable hybrids." In this model we are not the city's makers, or its authors, but its 'subjects'.[10] This take on the city, not as an object, but as a network – a mutable, flexible system that thrives on hybridity – is one that Stanisic pursues. Whilst Stanisic's conceptual framework of the city addresses specific pragmatics not so obviously present in the theories of Koolhaas, this energetic account of the city is important. The fixity of the approach of planners, developers and architects to the city is one that Stanisic sees as problematic for the growth of a sustainable city, and he asserts that one of the central problems with current strategies for Sydney's collective housing is a "distinct lack of typological investigation and transformation." The typical apartment tower "stacks environmentally mute containers on top of each other," which are capped with a figurative roof form, a nostalgic gesture to domesticity and as a symbol of dwelling. Stanisic further observes, "The contemporary city is full of contradictions, interrupted strategies and urban pathologies that offer unique opportunities for new projects, and which require an openness of mind to respond decisively, and with sensitivity. Our practice is concerned with exploring a number of key ideas and recurring themes, relating to the evolution of sites and programs."

Stanisic's research on typology led him to Anthony Vidler and his seminal essay *'The Third Typology'*.[11] Although written over three decades ago, Vidler argues a not dissimilar position to Koolhaas, that the city be accepted as is, thus serving as a 'locus of concern' and a source of architectural form.[12] This essay, one of a series of publications that revived the discussion of typology during in the 1960s and 70s, emerged in response to the supposed failure of the modern movement and its perceived disruption to the city. Italian architects and critics Aldo Rossi and Giulio Carlo Argan questioned how the city could be regenerated without functionalism, and without recourse to nostalgic ideas of the 'radiant city image' proposed by then contemporary urbanists. These theorists argued for a reconstitution of the city via type rather than program.

Vidler's vision of architectural typology avoids a romanticised idea of nature with affiliations to the primitive hut, or an industrialised model based on the machine and scientific rationalism. Architecture, and more specifically, building types should evolve from the fragments and continuities of the city itself. This was a plea against institutionalised abstract typologies that forged separation from, rather than connection to, the fabric and character of the city. As with Koolhaas, Vidler argues that "the city should be considered as a whole – a new typology in itself – with past and present revealed in its physical structure."[13] The typology Vidler proposed, and which Stanisic found so compelling – as demonstrated in such early projects as Atlas and Mondrian – was a model based on fragments of the city reassembled according to three "levels of meaning or conditions." Firstly, context is acknowledged, and meaning is taken from the "past existence of the form." Secondly, the specific site of the fragment – its boundaries, specific conditions, and the various types spanned across and between – constitutes another condition. Thirdly, the fragments are then "recomposed into a new context." Importantly, there is no stated or complete fit between form and use, as "typology defies a one to one reading of function, but… ensures a relation at another level to a continuing tradition of city life."[14] The essentially public character of architecture is given priority, and Vidler proposes that there is no 'clear set of rules for the transformations and their objects.' The inherent

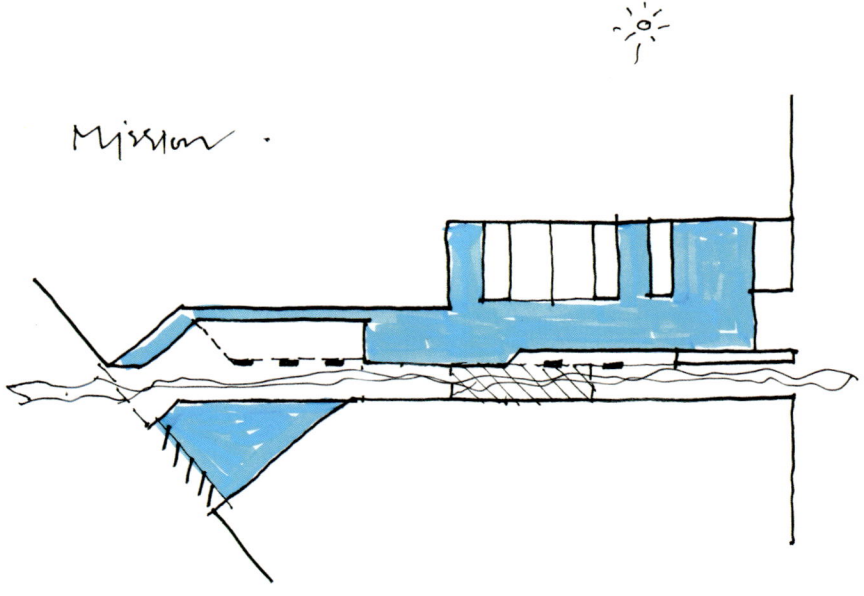

flexibility of what such architecture can be, with its critical and social purpose intact, allows for the evolution of an architecture that is of the city whilst being able to accommodate change. This is relevant for the later work of Stanisic Associates, which has become increasingly abstract and 'diagrammatic' in the clarity and the flexibility by which program, use and form are brought together.

The typological investigations of Stanisic Associates occur not only between the building and the city, but also within the building: type is considered at the scale of the building itself. The components of the building – access, circulation, organisation of living spaces, and outdoor spaces – are in themselves types through which we can understand the architectural intention. Typological investigation – rethinking what type means for architecture and for collective housing – is central to this practice's vision of a sustainable city: a discussion that increasingly prevails amongst those working internationally at the cutting edge of collective housing design. In their book *Typology +: Innovative Residential Architecture*,[15] the authors Peter Ebner et al observe that "the residential building viewed as a suit tailored to the subjective desires of the occupants is a relatively recent phenomenon in the history of housing." In its current incarnation, the house is unsustainable as a type, as is the house designed for the specific individual with specific needs and tastes. Residential buildings are being considered once again as a typological phenomenon. A central tenet of this argument is that genuine type possesses "a degree of universality and anonymity that can be used by others, by the discipline in general."[16]

Lieven De Boeck's work *'Seven Sins of Urbanism'*, shown in the exhibition *Negation in Art and Architecture*, held in Amsterdam in May 2005,[17] outlined a strategy for rethinking typologies and urbanism. Following on from Vidler, he argues that form be disconnected from dogmatic functionalism, and the type he proposes is one, like those of Stanisic Associates, that is diagrammatic – literally an abstract diagram – and inherently 'generative' within its framework. Resonating with Stanisic's conception of typology and his assertion of form as a framework for a multiplicity of occupations and events, De Boeck's model of type is of a flexible tool that is non-functional and informative rather than formal: he looks back to the Enlightenment for the initial iterations of type and architecture, to the proposal by Quatremre de Quincy in 1825 for a formless type, which was described as "a nucleus for a complexity of spatial arrangements that are adaptable to, but not (or not only) generated by function."[18]

Typological Invention at Millers Point: 1910-1918 and the Local Influences

Until recently, apartments rarely achieved the same level of architectural acclaim in Australia as the free standing house, and the prospects were even more remote if the project was low-cost social housing. Thus the significant work undertaken by William H. Foggitt working in the NSW Government Architect's Department between 1910 and 1918, has been largely ignored, apart from a mention in Butler-Bowden and Picket's *Homes in the Sky: Apartment Living in Australia*, although architect and academic Peter John Cantrill is keen to redress the oversight. Foggitt's inventive and economical collective housing and hybrid developments at Millers Point form one of the local starting points for the work of Stanisic Associates. Having endured a bubonic plague for the third time in 1900, The Rocks area to the northwest of the city centre was deemed unliveable by the Government who – not without realising the economic advantages – resumed the surrounding land and planned an extensive redevelopment of the Millers Point wharf precinct, which would include housing, shops and public amenities for the workers.

The state government of the time was a progressive one, and in addition to establishing a series of new institutions, including the first free kindergarten in 1906 and Government owned health clinics, they set up the first Housing Board. Adequately funded and well supported, this development, as Cantrill points out, "possessed perfect conditions for typological investigation and invention."[19] Two external directives tempered the appearance of what were essentially several variations of walk-up housing. Firstly, the development was designed to look like a row of terrace houses, rather than apartments, and secondly, there should be no evidence that any excessive money had been spent on the construction. Each terrace, appearing like one large federation house with a centrally placed door, was in fact comprised of four apartments. The architectural style, as Cantrill points out, was severe, rather bland, and certainly not in competition with the highly ornate and stylised apartments built contemporaneously at Elizabeth Bay and Potts Point. This simplicity, however, masked well-planned and well-built housing, which utilised high quality brickwork. The planning was innovative, as was the construction: a dwelling with a terrace house plan contained four one-storey flats vertically stacked and paired around an external stair, so that every dwelling had windows on three sides with a narrow courtyard in-between. Another type used an external corridor for access, and crossover planning made use of the stepped topography in a four-storey building. These apartments, accessed as two above the corridor and two below, were well ventilated and had a roof terrace for drying clothes.

According to Cantrill, another series of hybrid variations, dating from 1917, were located on Lower George Street, and comprised a shop on the ground floor level, a workshop on the first floor, and inhabitation on top. The access system – an external stair with lockable doors – allowed the building to be occupied in a variety of ways, with tenants taking a floor each, or one family occupying all three: making their goods on the upper floors and selling them below. Set on a sloping site, the buildings had a stepped section with a courtyard roofed by a glass skylight, which drew natural light into the middle of the workshop. Another example from 1917 saw the redevelopment of a complete city block with a mixed-use program and was, as Cantrill observes, a remarkable precedent for Stanisic's architecture. An infant health clinic and workshops were placed on the ground floor with shops

opposite page : Russian Constructivist 'crossover' section

19 Peter John Cantrill is a director at Tzannes Associates, where he has been employed for almost twenty years. He has conducted extensive research, published and taught on the urban design history of Sydney. He has been compiling previously unpublished material that documents Sydney's early apartments and mixed-use typological experiments. Cantrill was interviewed by Anna Johnson in July 2010.

20 Khan-Magomedov, Selim Omarovich, *Pioneers of Soviet Architecture*, Rizzoli International Publications, New York, 1987, p271

on each corner, and the block possessed at least five different apartment configurations. The block, adorned with a unified, relatively simple street façade, did not express the diversity of use to the street. Stanisic says of this development that "the complexity was there and supported the social complexity of the city, but the building also supported the street." Cantrill adjudges that these experiments were all largely ignored "until Frank Stanisic came along to continue these experiments of great value for the city, and for a broad cross section of the community."

Typological Invention in the Soviet Union and Europe: The International Influences.

The architecture of Stanisic Associates, seen especially in its refinement of the crossover type apartment configuration, draws direct inspiration from the work of the Russian Constructivists. Both the formal experiments – a now iconic architectural language of linear industrial abstractions punctuated by rhythms of glazing and structure – and the explorations of collective and social housing intrigued Stanisic, who admits that his crossover section can be traced back to "Ginzburg, Strioken and Ivonoff in the 1920s." The early planning and aesthetics of his practice were drawn from "the long thin slabs and cantilevers, and the collective public spaces embedded within the building" of the Constructivist work. Whilst the architectural expression of Stanisic's later work is less referential to that Constructivist language (it is now more preoccupied with an abstract tectonic, expressed as a perforated skin that wraps form), the crossover sectional arrangements of the Russians remain central.

The early years of Soviet architecture were characterised by a commitment to town planning, which aimed to accommodate a diversity of events, programs and social spaces.[20] The

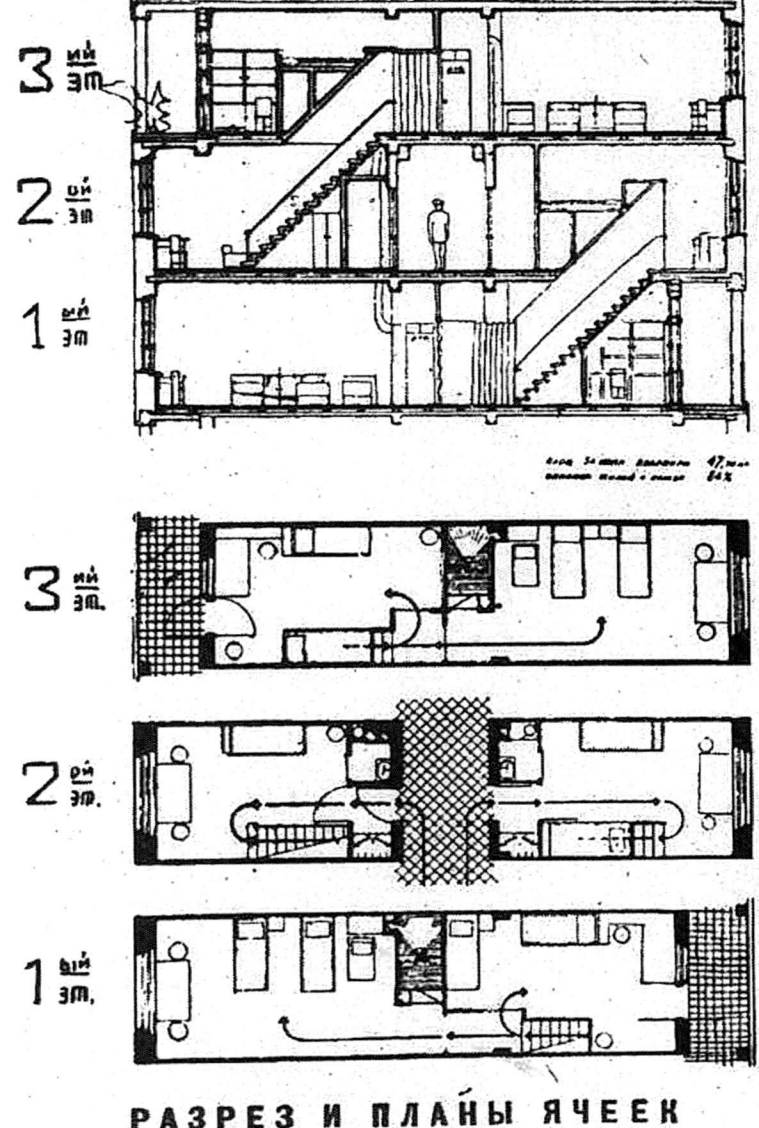

tone of this period was, despite the strictures of the Socialist system, 'multilateral'. Buildings were designed with flexible arrangements of planning and communal centres, and entire city buildings were vertically zoned. Following the October Revolution of 1917, architects were directed to create alternative forms of 'social' accommodation that would help establish the new way of life. Considerable investment went into making these dwellings (known as housing communes) comfortable, with access to shared public and cultural facilities in the development. Whilst the first half of the 1920s was a prolific time of experimentation, the acute shortage of housing in the mid 1920s, and some doubts about the completely communal housing models, led to experimentations of mass building methods and a more economically viable type of dwelling, which have influenced subsequent generations of architects.[21] The type that evolved became known as 'Sectional Housing', and comprised dwellings grouped around staircases, with two or three rooms over two levels wrapping a centrally enclosed corridor. These dwellings and their variations increased room size and ventilation, and provided individual access points to fresh air and vegetation.

Frank Stanisic studied a communal building designed by Moisei Ginzburg in 1927, which consisted of two six-storey dwelling blocks linked at the top by a communal component that held a canteen, a library, a reading room, a club and an assembly hall. The ground floor of each block included small annexes for children, with a kindergarten and crèche surrounding the stairs, with corridors, which ran between split-level apartments, providing internal communication and natural ventilation throughout the dwellings. Stanisic also studied the six experimental dwellings proposed for construction in 1930 in Moscow, Sverdlovsk, and Saratov, and he considered the most significant to be Ginzburg's Narkomfin building (designed in collaboration with Milinis between 1928 and 1930 in Moscow), which included apartments with communal and shopping facilities. The 'social condenser,' as this building became known, was the central precedent for Le Corbusier's Unité d'Habitation, Marseille (1946-52).

The Unité, with single- and two- level apartments enclosing a central corridor placed at every third level, is arguably the most famous – certainly the most published – example of the crossover sectional typology. Raised on *piloti*, with public green space intended to flow underneath the building, the rooftop supported a roof garden, a gym, a health care centre and a kindergarten. This was Le Corbusier's first opportunity to build his *machine á habiter*: his basic prototype for a green high-rise city with with vertically integrated services, amenities and recreation. The sectional configuration enabled double exposure for each apartment, natural ventilation, double-height living spaces and a variety of apartment configurations. The perforated concrete 'screen' – or *brise soleil* – developed by Le Corbusier as a shading device, worked to make the program legible, as well as adding a fine-grained texture and relief to large-scale concrete buildings. In Le Corbusier's building for the Quartier de la Marine (Algiers, 1938-42), the *brise-soleil* was integrated into the structural system, creating a woven density of light and shade, as well as maintaining unity across multiple scales.[22] In other projects, such as his unbuilt multi-purpose block for Nemours (Algeria, 1934), the *brise-soleil* is given depth, to form deep loggias and verandahs. In the work of Stanisic Associates, the integration of the *brise-soleil* can be detected in the early Domain and Mondrian buildings, and was utilised by the practice to provide an external reading of the buildings' interiors. The northern façade of Zone recalls most directly the geometric abstracted rhythm of the concrete *brise-soleil*, and as with the Unité d'Habitation, the depths are calculated to admit the winter sun and to protect the apartments from the summer glare. In more recent buildings, such as EDO, Coda and Era, the *brise-soleil* becomes more of a structure that supports a layering of screens, structure, outdoor spaces and louvred glazing, which Stanisic refers to as the "environmental screen." This threshold between interior and exterior performs as the dominant operable element, allowing individual occupants to control light, airflow and degrees of privacy.

The evolution of an unadorned and abstract architectural language in the work of Stanisic Associates clearly reveals the practice's affinity with 20th century modernist architecture, and the references are quite particular. A movement referred to as *Die Neue Sachlichkeit* (the New Objectivity) emerged from Germany after World War I, although some architects were already working in this style before the war as part of the *Deutscher Werkbund*. Stanisic's interest in this work, especially the Fagus Factory (Alfeld an der Leine, 1911) by Walter Gropius and Adolf Meyer, can be seen in Stanisic Associates' Mondrian project. Apart from the unadorned and abstract tectonics – informed more by structure and use than figuration and historical reference – the clear social objectives and collective housing initiatives of *Die Neue Sachlichkeit* are relevant for Stanisic Associates, and for contemporary Australia as a whole, as there has been minimal investment in collective housing, and in formal solutions that don't resort to nostalgic domestic references or a thinly veiled pastiche of form and colour. The flat roofs, the access to gardens, and the balconies of the apartments

opposite page : Mondrian, Waterloo, 2001-2002

21. Khan-Magomedov, Selim Omarovich, 1987, p346

22. William J. R. Curtis, *Le Corbusier: Ideas and Forms*, Phaidon, 2nd Edition, London, 1992, p118

23. Wallis Miller, 'IBA's "Models for a City": Housing and the Image of Cold-War Berlin', in *Journal of Architectural Education* (1984-), Vol. 46, No. 4, (May, 1993), Association of Collegiate Schools of Architecture, Inc. p204

of Bruno Taut's Prenzlauer Estate (Berlin, 1927) illustrate the *Existenzminimum* creed of *Die Neue Sachlichkeit*: to provide all Germans with 'a healthy dwelling', achieved with minimally acceptable floor space, efficient density levels, fresh air, and proximity to green space and public amenities. It is from these histories that Stanisic has derived his own design platform of 'Eco Minimalism', an approach that reconciles sustainability – the environmental response – with what Stanisic calls an "appropriate modernism." This agenda (or platform) is, he explains, "a reaction to the more conventional responses to ecological design, where the building must overtly demonstrate its greenness with materials and an aesthetic that immediately register it as an ecological environmentally responsive building." Stanisic implements such passive design principles as airflow, solar access and orientation with a construction system that uses embodied materials to "produce a building that is quite abstract and restrained, and which becomes more minimal in its expression."

Berlin Internationale Bauaustellung and Green Square

In 1996, Frank Stanisic was selected as a finalist in the international Green Square Ideas Competition, which called for a major renewal of the 275 hectare South Sydney brownfield area. His winning Green Square Structural Masterplan of 1998 was based on a vision of an environmentally sustainable neighbourhood, which supported the wellbeing of present and future communities, and provided a complex environment for encouraging social interaction. The masterplan, unprecedented in its scope for Sydney, had a population projection of 25,000 living and 15,000 working in the precinct. The idea, predicated on three concepts of 'diversity', 'connectivity', and 'interdependency', began with Stanisic's observations of the neighbouring, somewhat untidy but vibrant, mixed-use suburb of Surry Hills, the area where he had been born and grew up, and next to Erskineville where he worked with his father during school holidays making float glass 'on the tanks' at the ACI glassworks.

The large scale and complexity of the Green Square project would prove to be critical for Stanisic Associates as they developed and solidified their ideas about the city and collective housing, and it also provided the opportunity for the practice to design many mixed-use residential buildings. The courtyard blocks that formed the basic type for the Green Square Masterplan were transformed from European courtyard blocks by a clear focus on climatic response, courtyard permeability, hybrid uses, crossover design, abstract form and industrial expression. The courtyard became the essential organising element of each site, and was to mutate into its many forms in Stanisic's completed projects: finger, quadrangle, multi-level, irregular, triangular, linear, terrace, split and elevated, each responding to the specifics of each site.

Very few, if any, local precedents existed, and Stanisic looked overseas for relevant models. The recently completed IBA (*Internationale Bauaustellung* or International Building Exhibition, 1979-87) in Berlin became one of the practice's key precedents: as Stanisic recalls, "The IBA was the best global example of the development and transformation of the modern city." The genesis of the IBA had begun in 1970 with the discussion for an ideas competition to produce designs for the redevelopment of Tiergarten, an area adjoining the Landwehrkanal in the centre of Berlin, which had once contained the city's embassies and its central park. The precinct had become marginalised after World War II and the partition of Berlin, and now housed the city's poor and destitute. The ambitions of the competition expanded to strengthen West Berlin's global image and to attract new residents to the city, whilst improving the lot of the existing inhabitants. The IBA became a twofold project: to provoke ideas and discussions that would generate models rather than a model for the city, which would demonstrate the intellectual image and diversity of Berlin; and to provide subsidised housing that could accommodate a diversity of occupants and lifestyles. Although the scope of the IBA also embraced the planning of city administration buildings, and social and technical infrastructure, it was to be the

opposite page : model photographs of Green Square Masterplan

24 Wallis Miller, 1993, p206
25 Wallis Miller, 1993, p212

subsidised housing that conveyed the IBA's inner-city alternatives and West Berlin's new image to the public.[24] Although many of the IBA designs were little more than architecturally varied and expressive façade designs that cloaked relatively conventional housing types and interior layouts,[25] many projects demonstrated typological invention and saw the modification of Europe's traditional perimeter type housing blocks. Some developments also integrated passive solar systems, and created more complex relationships between interior and exterior spaces, as well as between public and private thresholds. The IBA climaxed with the urban renewal of Potsdamer Platz, a mixed-use precinct, of streets, blocks and public spaces adjacent to the Berlin Wall.

In its totality, the IBA represented an archetypical European approach to the rebuilding of the inner city, and reinforced the position that the implementation of social housing is tantamount to the creation of an inner city fabric and identity. This richness of debate and the large-scale testing of ideas intrigued Stanisic, and he spent much time and resource studying the city and the project, as well as Berlin's many other historic urban housing projects. As he points out, the IBA was premised upon a perimeter type, which reinstated the street: a block edge development that enclosed a central courtyard, not a common type in Sydney, but one that formed the starting point for the Green Square proposal. However, as he observed, the continuous perimeter – often poorly orientated, and needlessly segregating the dwelling and its internal courtyard from the street – needed strategic modifications. The transformation Stanisic Associates made was to break that block, thus improving orientation whilst introducing different uses and programs at street level. In the Atlas and Mondrian developments, a

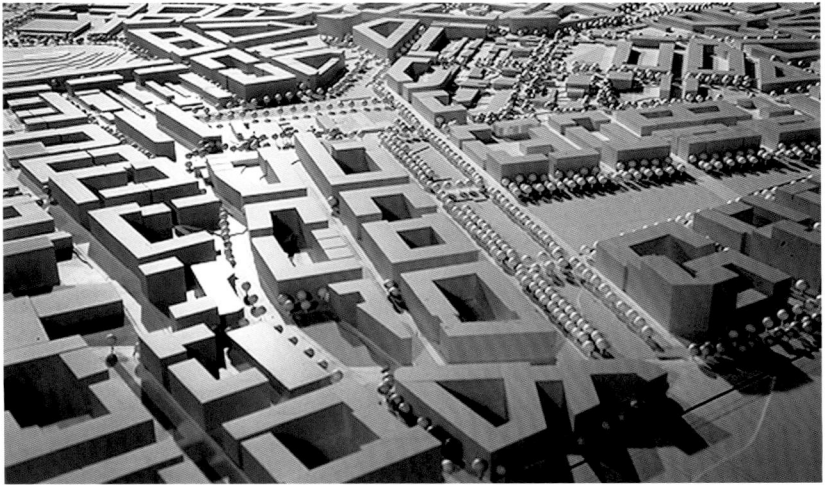

permeable block – punctuated with through-site access – is utilised to activate the street condition, and supplies a physical, environmental and visual continuity from street to courtyard. At Mondrian, the model is fragmented further to become a series of smaller blocks orientated so that all buildings receive northern light and enclose a series of smaller 'finger' type courtyard gardens. The design actively connects to existing site conditions and streets, and serves to make the ground plan a more varied texture of public, private and semi-private spaces, in keeping with the fabric of a city.

Removing the Artificial Support System

Contemporary architects are natural and necessary participants in the debates concerning climate change, the desirability of achieving zero carbon emissions in buildings and cities, and the sustainable management of increasing densities. Whilst questions of aesthetics and appearance remain significant for Stanisic, his enquiries have been supplemented by questions of environmental sustainability and passive design. His approach is to apply comparatively 'low tech', well-planned passive design solutions, rather than to work through a scientific checklist. He refers to the unplugged environment that has, within its systems and structure, the ability to behave much like a naturally breathing body. After Domain received the inaugural NSW Premier's Award for Residential Design, Stanisic's early projects – extensively illustrated in the NSW Residential Flat Design Code (RFDC), relating to the State Environmental Planning Policy (SEPP 65) – have become touchstones for the design of medium and high density housing in Australia.

The spatial experiential atmospheres created within his buildings have been achieved without the need for "artificial support systems," as Stanisic describes them. Airflow and orientation are central to this, and Stanisic's buildings, with their careful orientation of sunny northern sides and cooler southern sides, produce the temperature differentials needed to facilitate the natural movement of air throughout the interiors. The northern elevation becomes an operable and permeable environmental threshold, or skin, that combines sun shading with protected extensive balconies and glazing: access and circulation are located on the shaded southern side.

Stanisic has evolved several circulation access types and crossover apartment arrangements to facilitate cross ventilation. Mondrian marks a critical point in this refinement of passively designed collective housing, with an ensemble of slimline building blocks enclosing 'finger' courtyards, precast concrete building technology, and an implementation of crossover planned apartments, unprecedented in Sydney. Coda, however, is a single tall slim building on a prominent corner site that achieves passive design efficiency through open access galleries and crossover planning, and marks an evolution in the treatment of the northern façade with a threshold that performs as what Stanisic terms an "environmental screen." This threshold is a three-metre-deep section that comprises double-height plantation shutters, multi-folding panels and timber decked double-height 'sunroom' balconies accessed through sliding doors and louvred windows. The next iteration was to be seen with EDO, a building that demonstrated the evolution of several significant strategies, and where Stanisic's intention to create a framework for 'atmospheres' – a framework for dwelling – is most obviously expressed. An open two-storey-high mezzanine access gallery draws in cool air from the eastern garden through fixed open louvres, which then flows through operable louvres located above the apartment entry doors into the apartments on the building's western side. The internal

opposite page : EDO, Woolloomooloo, 2005-2007

planning of each apartment is flexible and responsive with the application of slide-away translucent walls, beds that can be folded away, and rooms that can be opened up for alternative modes of living or social requirements. At Era, a seven-storey work/shop building, the gallery circulation is transformed to create an open breezeway that runs between the two central building volumes. This covered public throughway can be seen as a transformation of the traditional Sydney arcade type – a vertical array of floors lined with shops – to a passively designed breezeway with gallery walkways for pedestrian access to offices. Enclosed by fine metal gridded screens at either end and roofed with stepping glass louvres, this breezeway operates as a thermal stack, which encourages cool breezes to travel through the space and into the offices.

Future Trajectories and New Imperatives.

For Stanisic Associates, housing and its hybrid variations cannot not be relegated to the periphery of the city: the city does not begin where the housing ends or vice versa, but is wrapped around, through, and with, this typology. Significantly, this type can no longer be seen as 'housing', but as a hybrid variation designed by architects who offer alternatives to current planning regulations and criteria. Traditionally, housing has provided a catalyst for change, and now is the time for architects to take the initiative and to demonstrate through example what that change will be. Housing is now required to increase the density of the city, whilst establishing new relationships between public and private, the home and the street, and between the environment and society.

In *Public Housing and Space: A Manifesto*,[26] Juan Herreros writes "…it is difficult to know when the architectural project rejected the communal uses of collective housing. Even more difficult to comprehend, is the reluctance to develop mixed-use typologies that include the participation of residential public use." Architecture and urban design have grown apart – they now exist as two distinct and separate professions – but the sustainability of the city calls for them to be immediately reintegrated, and for the practitioners to look to economists, developers and environmental engineers to work collaboratively. The future of the city, and of the lifestyle of its people, lie in a more integrated field of research, where the form of the buildings is, on the one hand, an environmentally responsive container, but on the other, can be generative and suggestive, rather than tied to historical ideas of predetermined function and use.

Javier Mozas and Aurora Fernandez Per, authors of *Density: New Forms of Collective Housing*,[27] list several possibilities for the evolution of the house type: a car-free house, a flexible house, an assisted living house, and a green house, to name just a few. These architects propose that "the house of the future will be an office: an office where one sleeps and sometimes, only sometimes, one cooks. It will be a hotel in which all ancillary services will be taken care of." However, as a permutation of the future, and as something that Stanisic Associates are actively pursuing, the proposition that architecture is a flexible system connected to the life of the city, and to the micro-environment of the immediate context, is crucial.

The next evolution and the future trajectories of Stanisic Associates, as expressed in Era and such unbuilt projects as Roseville and Hyperform, are increasingly concerned with ideas of hybridity and compactness. The architecture becomes a compact interwoven system of program, and public and outdoor spaces. Form is therefore increasingly abstract and flexible, and the tectonics, planning and general resolution are informed by a versatility of use and a highly responsive environmental shell: a container that operates to engage with and temper the environment. Outdoor spaces are embedded within the building, and public and

---

opposite page : Era, Kings Cross, 2005-2009

26 Juan Herreros of Abalos and Herreros, 'Public Housing and Space: A Manifesto' in *Collective Housing: A Manual*, Jose Maria de Lapuerta, ACTAR, Barcelona, 2007, p15

27 Javier Mozas and Aurora Fernandez Per, *Density: New Forms of Collective Housing*, a+t Editions, Vitoria-Gasteiz, 2006, p45

community interaction occurs not only within embedded public space, but also within the ancillary spaces of circulation and access. This type of microenvironment is what Stanisic describes as a 'loose fit, long life and low energy' typology (LF:LL:LE). Era is one example of this new direction: the building was initially designed and approved as collective housing, but the program was then changed to small offices (SOHO without the HO). As the building was conceived as a passive environmental container, with an active inside and outside relationship created by open access galleries and a breezeway running through its centre, it could easily function as a hybrid (i.e. live, work and shop). Services were also scaled back, but little change was required to the building's exterior due to the flexibility of this microenvironment.

Architecture that is increasingly compact and hybrid in program is demonstrated in the work of contemporary European architects – such as MVRDV, OMA and Neutelings in Holland, and BIG and CF Moller in Denmark – who are designing large scale, but very compact and self sufficient buildings that have regard and respect for the needs of both their immediate occupants and those of the surrounding city and streetscape. In China, Steven Holl has proposed what he calls a Sliced Porosity Block for Chengdu. These buildings, which satisfy a multitude of uses, and perform social and environmental roles, ironically possess a kind of formal freedom of expression, where tectonic resolution is not tied to specific ideas of program and use, and prioritises engagement with larger, more consequential ambitions, such as the relationship between culture, society and the city, and, most critically, with the sustainability of the environment. As Australian cities continue to grow, we will inevitably look to these types of projects as the solution to the issues of the 21st century, and the rigorous research and typological innovations of Stanisic Associates will provide the framework for this next generation of architecture.

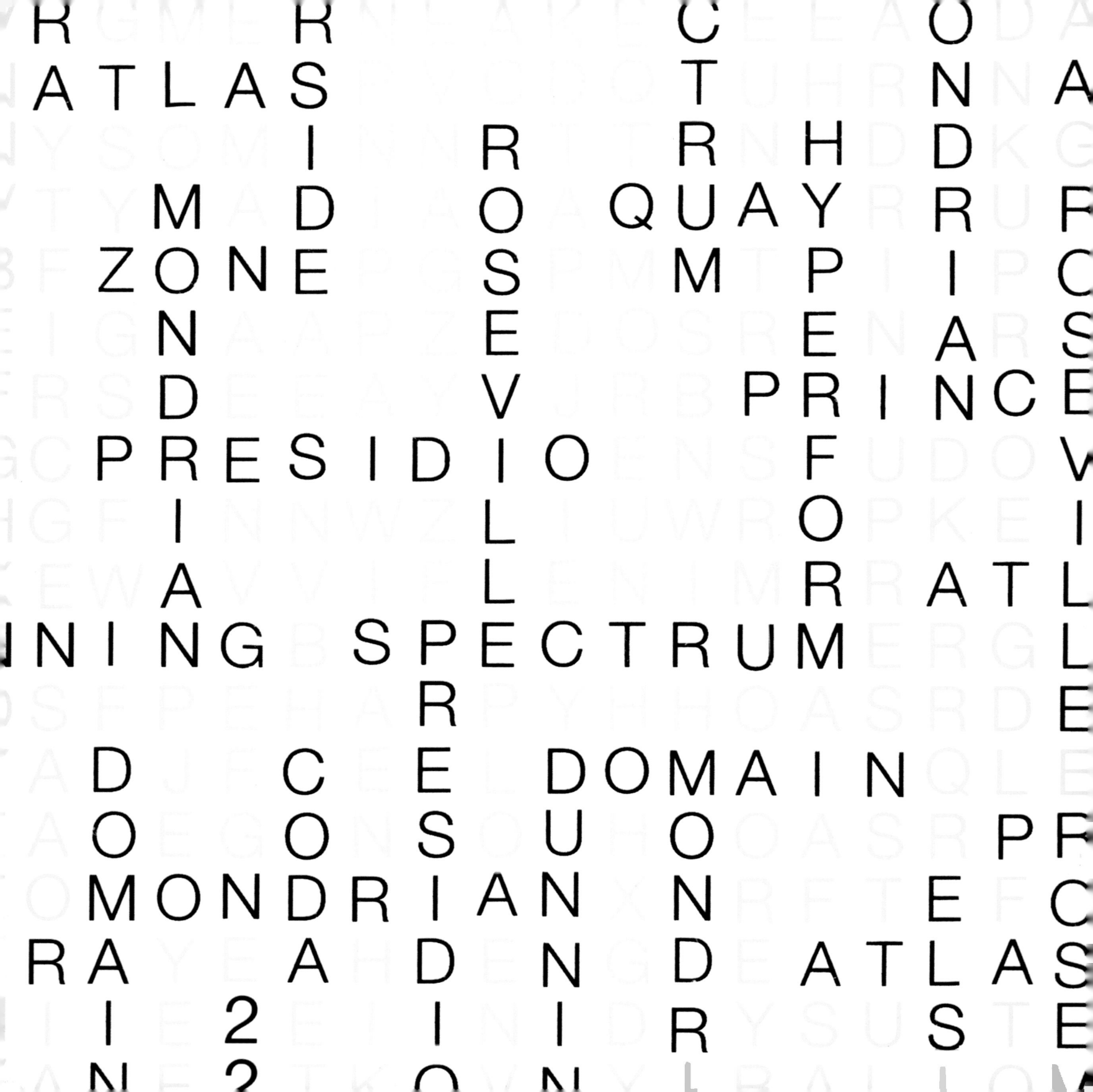

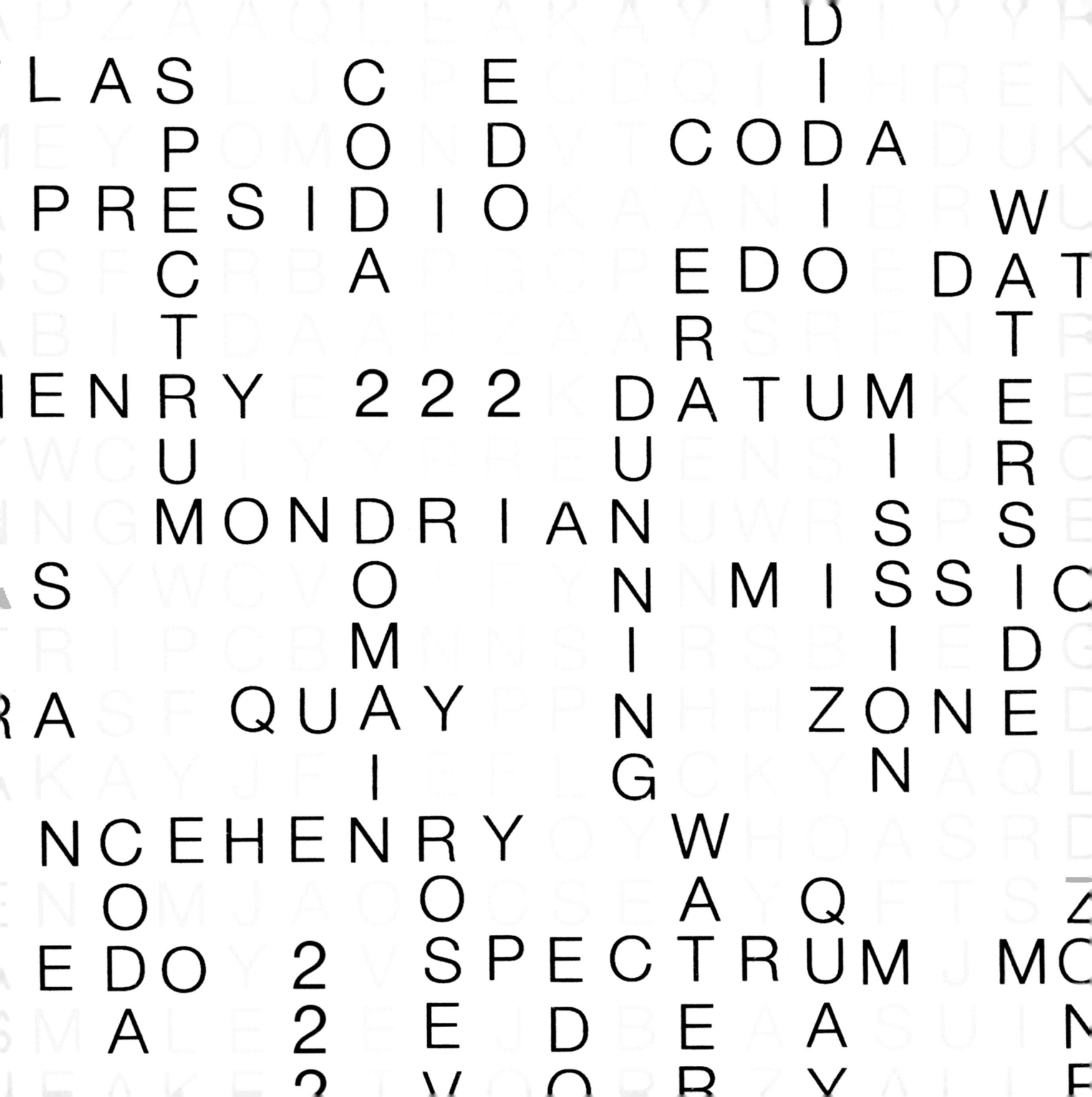

Marrickville 1998-2001

DOMAIN

A robust five-storey and decidedly modern building on a corner site, Domain is one of Stanisic Associates' earliest hybrid projects. An environmentally responsive mixed-use development was inserted into one of the main streets of the inner Sydney suburb of Marrickville: it was a proposal that established the practice as leaders in this evolving Sydney typology. Domain demonstrated that not only was it possible to place a contemporary elemental building – abstract and compositional – into a street dominated by Victorian era low-scale shopfronts, but that such a development would reactivate the street and add to the richness of the local precinct. Whilst the architectural language employed is not as disciplined or refined as the architects' later projects, it clearly articulates an urban agenda to bring living, shopping and working – 'live, shop, work' – into the same development. The aim was to create an active vibrant relationship between programs, and between the building and the streetscape. Most significantly, the architecture represents a clear departure from the then commonplace Sydney apartment buildings, which made overt reference to local context through gestures of figurative pastiche, and comprised a series of vertically stacked slabs without consideration for outdoor access, orientation or cross-ventilation: an architecture that Frank Stanisic describes as "the air-conditioned pancake typology."

Drawing on Stanisic's knowledge and first hand experience of the IBA collective housing project in Berlin, and his fascination with the conceptual housing projects of the early Russian Constructivists,

view from northeast

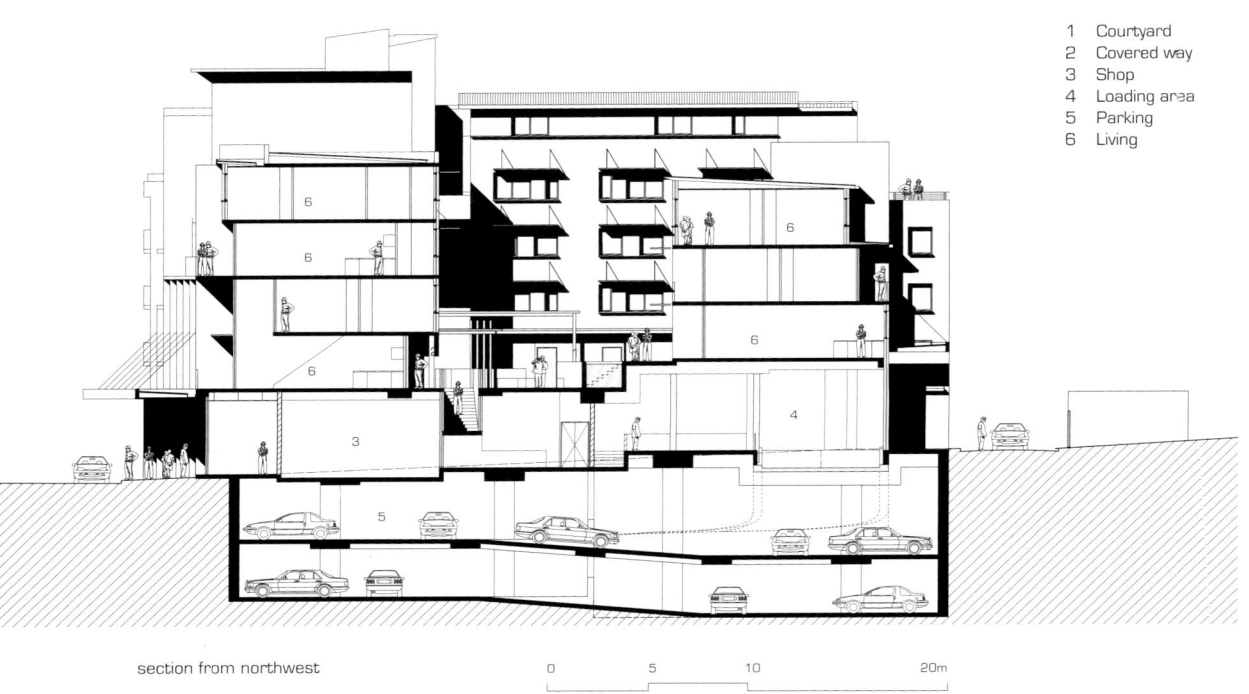

1 Courtyard
2 Covered way
3 Shop
4 Loading area
5 Parking
6 Living

section from northwest

the formal arrangement of the Domain project consists of three connected perimeter buildings enclosing a courtyard. Shops and offices are placed at street level, below the apartments, and in response to the specific heights of the surrounding context and in order to avoid overshadowing, the building heights vary from four storeys to seven storeys at the corner.

Although the tectonics are abstracted, planar and robust, with no ornamentation, a careful contextual dialogue is established through these broader formal gestures and then through the layered articulation of balconies, windows and setbacks. The 'street wall' building on Marrickville Road is five storeys high, but a setback at the third floor continues the parapet line of the existing shops. This 'datum' establishes an alternate rhythm between the darkly rendered lift cores, the cellular concrete blades that define each two-storey apartment, and the assemblage of sunshades, balconies and windows. Yellow and orange tones mark out the lobby, lifts and public entries, contrasting with the dominant colour palette of greys, purple and dark blue: reinforcing the intentional expression of the building's program.

north elevation

The apartments themselves are planned around two lift lobbies, access stairs, and a secure external courtyard. All apartments – a mixture of predominantly two-level apartments, lofts and maisonettes – have generous north- and east-facing balconies and terraces. The comprehensive application of passive solar design initiatives, which eliminated the need for air-conditioning, includes cross-ventilation through the slender buildings, and access to well orientated outdoor spaces, whilst the bathrooms are located on exteriors walls to avoid mechanical ventilation. Aligned with a carefully designed courtyard and gallery circulation space, Domain is a very considered environmental response, critically positioned in the evolution of Stanisic Associates.

1 Courtyard
2 Covered way
3 Lobby
4 Gallery
5 Terrace
6 Living
7 Dining
8 Bedroom

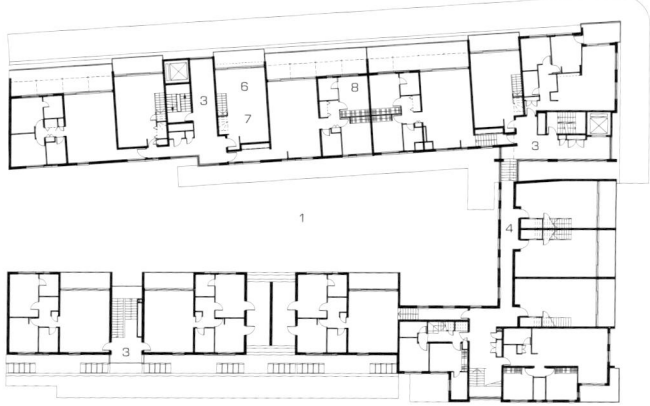

third floor plan

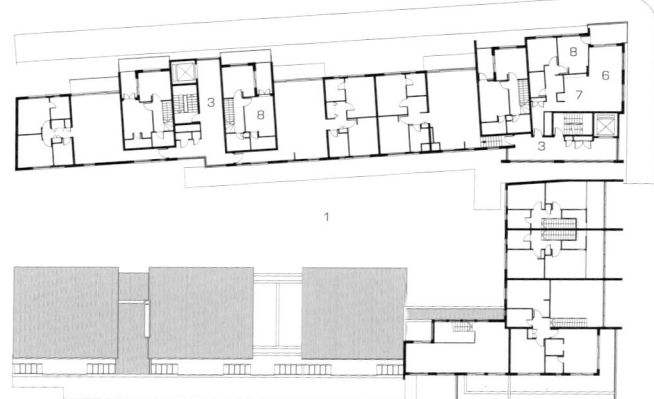

fourth floor plan

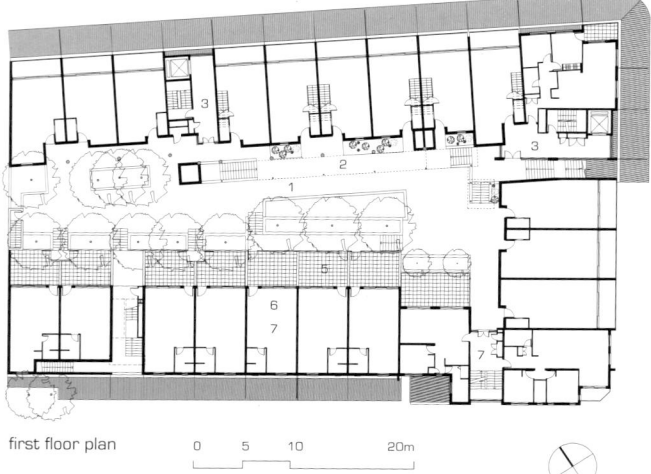

first floor plan

second floor plan

north elevation

Newtown 1998-2002
PRESIDIO

As with Domain in Marrickville, Presidio – located in the inner-west suburb of Newtown – is an early but significant project for Stanisic Associates. Whilst the materiality of the project – which Frank Stanisic refers to as "rail architecture," with timber louvres and plywood cladding at the higher levels – is a 'one off,' the planning, the use of a gallery system for circulation, and the ideas behind its conception, all form important precedents for later work. Located on a triangular site, adjacent to the railway station and King Street, and bounded by Erskineville Road and Brennan Lane, the site was beset by a series of difficult constraints, such as noise from nearby trains and cars, the heights of the adjacent terraces, limited vehicle access and circulation space, and a bland commercial development to the north. The development was therefore as much concerned with careful urban repair and renewal as it was with collective housing.

The arrangement of the two dominant buildings on the site was driven by the idea of a fragmented perimeter form, which encircles a central north-facing triangular courtyard. Whilst the architecture and the composition are muscular – the construction is largely concrete and rendered brick – the project possesses an ordered rhythmic aesthetic that expresses a cellular 'diagram' for the apartment configuration. In contrast to this, a delicate roof appears to float above the façades, and lightweight plywood sheeting is used to clad the topmost levels. The 'carriage-like' northern elevations, overlooking the courtyard, are animated by operable western red

north elevation from courtyard

above left and above : eastern block

1 Courtyard
2 Terrace
3 Living
4 Dining
5 Kitchen
6 Bedroom
7 Lobby
8 Gallery
9 Retail

ground floor plan   0 5 10 20 50m

north elevation

fourth floor plan

left, above and opposite : north elevation of western block

cedar sliding plantation shutters, which veil the sun-filled balconies. Defining the courtyard, and facing Erskineville Road and the railway line, these slender 'edge' and 'wedge' buildings (as they are called), hold 120 apartments in single- and double-storey configurations. The ground floor and street-facing elevations are activated by the addition of shops and a café, and the 'edge' building – a six-storey block adjacent to the railway – is planned so that the living spaces and outdoor balcony spaces face north, and overlook the courtyard. To the south, a more defensive protecting wall with glazed attachments shields the bedrooms from the railway, and operates to define the edge. Another string of courts, running along this southern wall, is protected by timber screens. The dwelling themselves are therefore nestled between perimeter balcony spaces, which allow for cross-ventilation, outdoor access, natural light, and further insulation from the noise.

In contrast, and in direct response to the adjacent urban context of Erskineville Road, the 'wedge' building is a more thickly modelled form that becomes a layered urban street wall with recessed balconies. This elevation holds the main entry, street level shops and a café. The building is set back 2.5 metres to allow for a widened footpath and cycleway, and the footpath itself was repaved and planted with trees. In an extension of its urban restorative role, this 'wedge' building acts as 'moderator' between the scales of terrace buildings along Erskineville Road and the larger commercial development on Brennan Road. Improvements were also made to the road width, footpaths, and an open space that forms part of the commercial development, whilst a through-site connection was made to the Newtown railway station at the western end of the project. Presidio, more than just a well-considered infill housing project, is also regenerative: site has been addressed in its entirety, as a system linked into the network of the inner city, resulting in a development that realises the site's potential, and amplifies Newtown's character and identity.

Alexandria 2000-2002

ATLAS

An early collective housing project, Atlas clearly reflects the perimeter courtyard typology that formed part of the research for the Green Square Master Plan, a competition for an urban renewal project of 275 hectares in the South Sydney area won by Frank Stanisic (in association with Hassell) in 1998. During this formative period, the office explored housing typologies for Sydney that would be environmentally responsive and well ventilated, and that would also address the difficult questions of urban context and appropriate streetscapes for these industrial brown-fill sites. At that time very few, if any, local models existed, so Stanisic looked abroad for precedent. Between 1983 and 1997, he had travelled to Europe and, most significantly, to Germany, where he studied the urban housing developments of the IBA – *Internationale Bauaustellung Berlin 1987* – an international building exhibition initiated by the West Berlin Parliament for the much needed reconstruction of Berlin. The IBA's predominant type, a perimeter building block enclosing a central courtyard, was a critical example for Stanisic.

Located on a generous site in Alexandria, adjacent to Green Square and opposite Alexandria Park, Atlas is bounded on three sides by offices and warehouses, and Stanisic's response was to 'reinstate the street' using a perimeter edge development. The four individual blocks were then detailed to respond to the immediate context and climatic condition of each orientation. Unlike the IBA examples, Stanisic breaks the continuity of the edge, thus establishing visual and environmental permeability between the building forms, the

east elevation

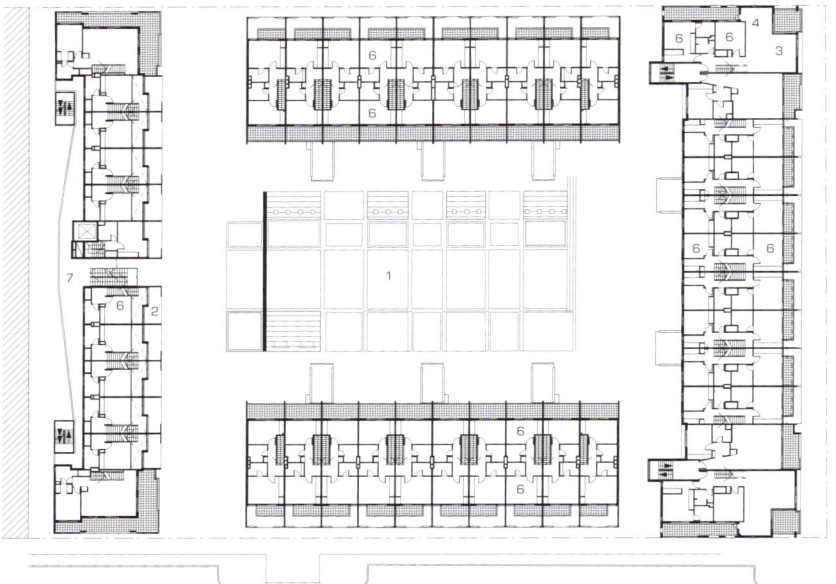

third floor plan

courtyard and apartments
from northwest

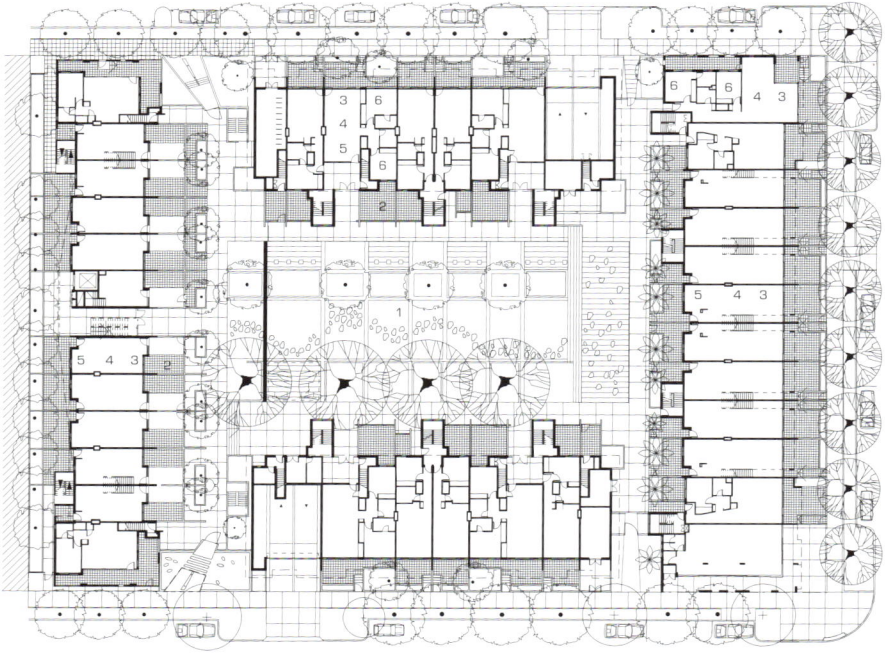

ground floor plan   0 5 10 20   50m

1 Courtyard
2 Terrace
3 Living
4 Dining
5 Kitchen
6 Bedroom
7 Gallery

left: north elevation
below: courtyard from southwest

central green courtyard and the street. The building blocks of four and five storeys contain 121 apartments of one, two and three bedrooms, in a mix of double- and single-storey dwellings, with car park and storage on a basement level that runs below the courtyard. All apartments have double orientation, and where possible have north-facing living and balcony spaces. Access and circulation, dependent upon on the block's orientation, is through a series of open and closed circulation galleries, and detached lift cores, whilst for the street-facing lower level apartments, access is directly from the street via stairs. Sydney's SEPP 65 planning and aesthetic regulations state that a courtyard width must be no less that the height of buildings: at 30 metres wide, the courtyard at Atlas – a rich varied landscape of raised garden beds, deciduous trees, grassed areas and seating – is more than twice that recommendation.

The north-facing elevation, on Power Avenue, establishes a strong visual edge to the park: a four-storey building, with two arrangements of double-storey terrace apartments, has a rhythm of blade walls, balconies and glazing that resonates with the nearby Victorian terraces. Bookending this elevation, the corners articulate the change of direction and a new climatic orientation. Corner balconies are introduced, whilst white-rendered masonry slabs and columns frame exposed face-brick surfaces. Typical of the practice's earlier projects, the architectural language is more pronounced, with changes in program creating articulated expression on the exterior. The roof is unusually expressive, with a saw-tooth profile that denotes the site's industrial history, and supplies an angled surface upon which solar panels have been installed. Sliding double-height aluminium plantation shutters protect these east- and west-facing blocks from the sun and, when read alongside the expressive roof profile, establish a tectonic language that reconciles their domestic program with the adjacent industrial warehouses.

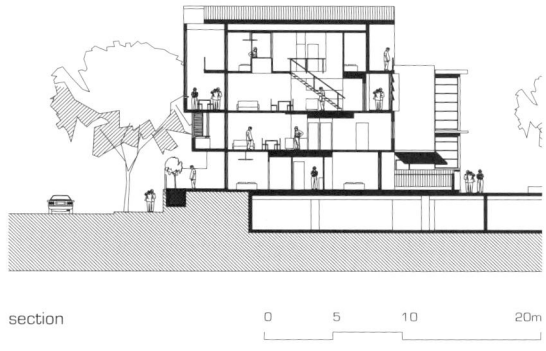

section

west elevation

Waterloo 2001-2002

MONDRIAN

Designed in the afterglow of the Sydney 2000 'green' Olympic Games, and demonstrating the potential of sustainable collective housing, Mondrian was a pivotal project for Stanisic Associates. The architects' pursuit of a robust architectural language is highly evident: a muscular, modern, and abstract tectonic, yet one that yields to its context and to its environment. Located in Waterloo, an industrial suburb with the highest number of public housing developments in Sydney, the project is the most environmentally responsive apartment building in the Green Square 'zone' and, at the time of completion, its eco-responsiveness, its efficient use of precast concrete building technology, and its adaptation of crossover planned apartments was unprecedented in Sydney. In the words of the architectural jury that awarded the project the RAIA Wilkinson Award in 2003, "This is delivered in a stunning and refined 'new modern script' that is a welcome antidote to much of the regressive nostalgia permeating our cities and suburbs."

Mondrian is also an expression of the key ideas underpinning the Green Square Master Plan, an urban renewal project of 275 hectares (the largest comprehensive urban redevelopment in Sydney to date) won, through international competition, by Frank Stanisic in 1998. The master plan's ideas of permeability, connectivity and interdependence inform the conceptual armature for Mondrian, and find expression at the scale of individual buildings and at the broader scale of the project's relationship with the site's public and infrastructural amenities. As Stanisic states, the vision of Green

north elevation

view from northeast

Square was to create a dynamic urban place, an inspirational and sustainable living and working environment for the 21st century and, importantly, one that fostered a new sensibility.

In a move away from previous projects, the perimeter edge buildings are fragmented to become a series of four buildings of between four to seven storeys each, with their own systems of access, light wells and circulation. The typical central courtyard was dispersed to become a series of green slim-line courtyards running between the apartments and connecting back to a central circulation spine. Although the net density achieved is remarkable – the equivalent of 500 persons per hectare – and at a cost of roughly $2200 per square metre, the site coverage is only 38 percent, leaving 62 percent of the ground plane as open public and private space. Importantly, the project is not an enclave: it encourages connectivity to parks and shops, and provides 24 hour public access between the two streets bounding the site.

All but three of the 132 apartments have north-facing living areas, garden courts, or generous balconies. The slender footprint of the apartment blocks – housing one-storey apartments, two-storey terraces, and maisonettes of one, two and three bedrooms – adopts the crossover planning section and gallery circulation systems

1 Through Site Link
2 Public Park
3 Finger Courtyard

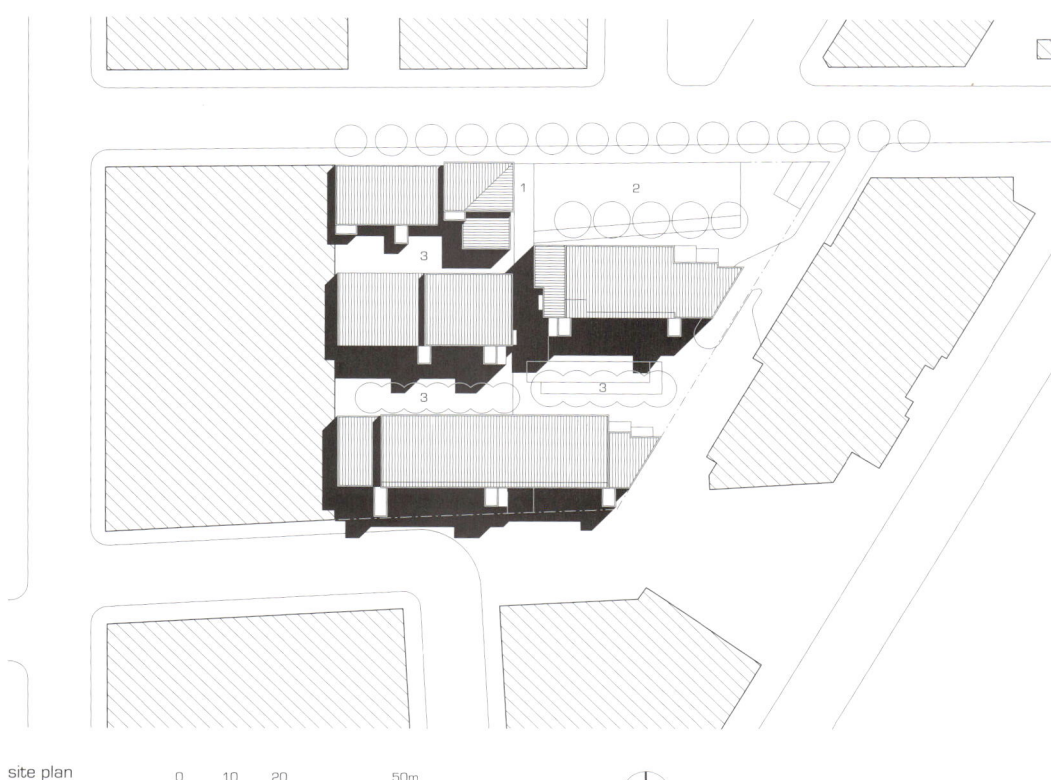

site plan

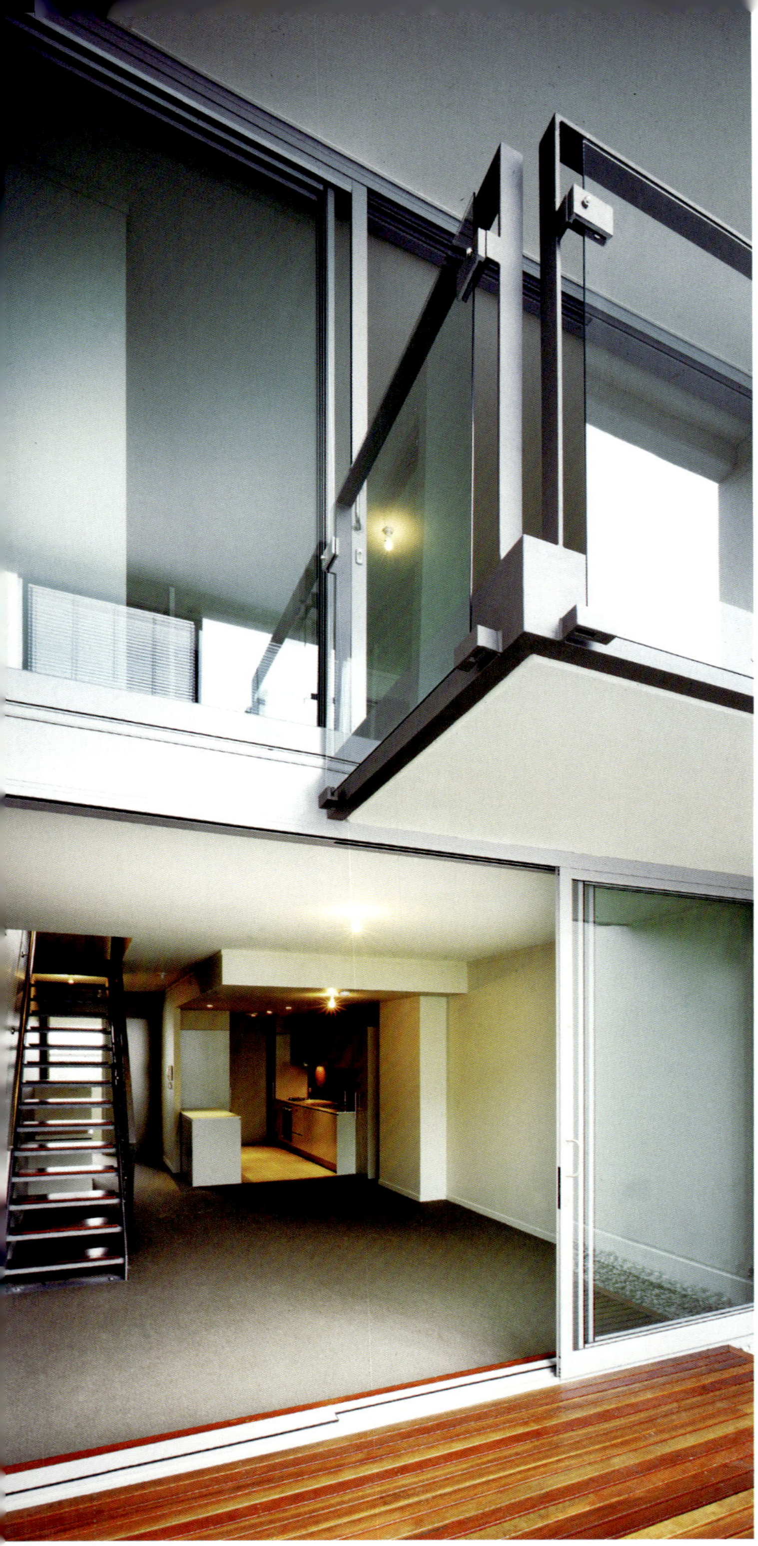

photograph © Brett Boardman

photograph © Brett Boardman

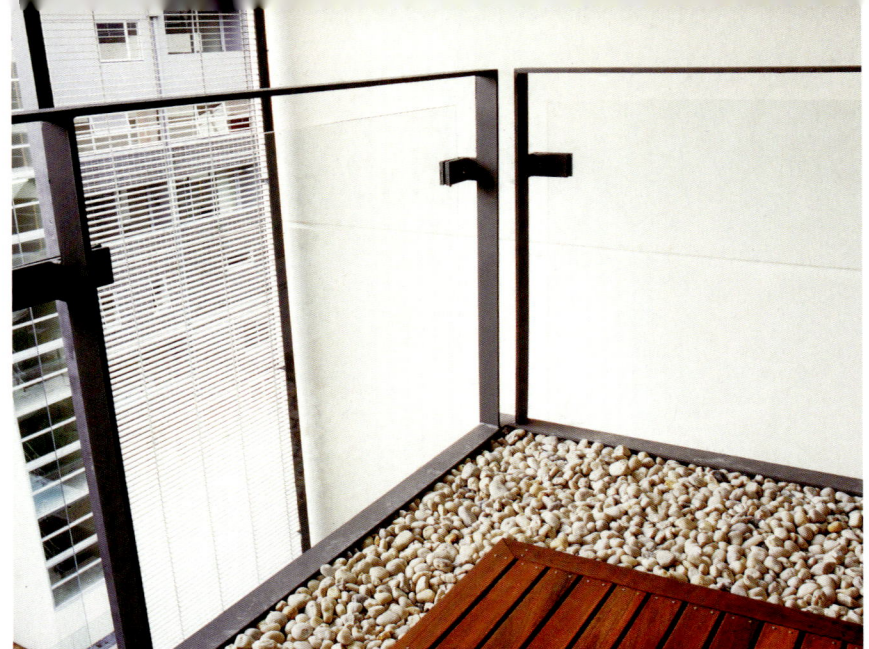

that the practice had been researching for several years. Spanning the width of its building, each apartment is orientated to take advantage of the temperature differential between the cooler southern side and the warm northern façade to generate cross-ventilation. No apartment requires air-conditioning, and double-loaded circulation corridors have been avoided.

Mondrian is also a direct expression of the architects' idea of an expanded permeable wall: operable and transparent to allow for direct climatic and environmental response. The northern façades read as crate-like *brises soleil* with deep balconies that draw in light and sun, and in combination with an external expression of each apartment type, creates layered muscular buildings that acknowledge – through a material ensemble of precast concrete, brick tiles and metal wall cladding – the thoroughly unromantic industrial context of Waterloo. Softening this aesthetic, spotted gum plantation decking and white Cowra river stones are used in each apartment, whilst delicate anodised sliding and fixed screens are used for privacy and climate control. As with most Stanisic Associates projects, and in common with the precedents that the work recalls (the expressive buildings of the Russian Constructivists and the direct economy of early European modernism from Walter Gropius to Le Corbusier) there are no iconic eye-catching waterside views or rich undulating topography. The architects work with uncompromising 'brown-fill' sites where delight must come directly from the architecture and from the responsive and inventive curation of site, environment, space and form.

above and opposite : typical apartment fitouts

photograph © Brett Boardman

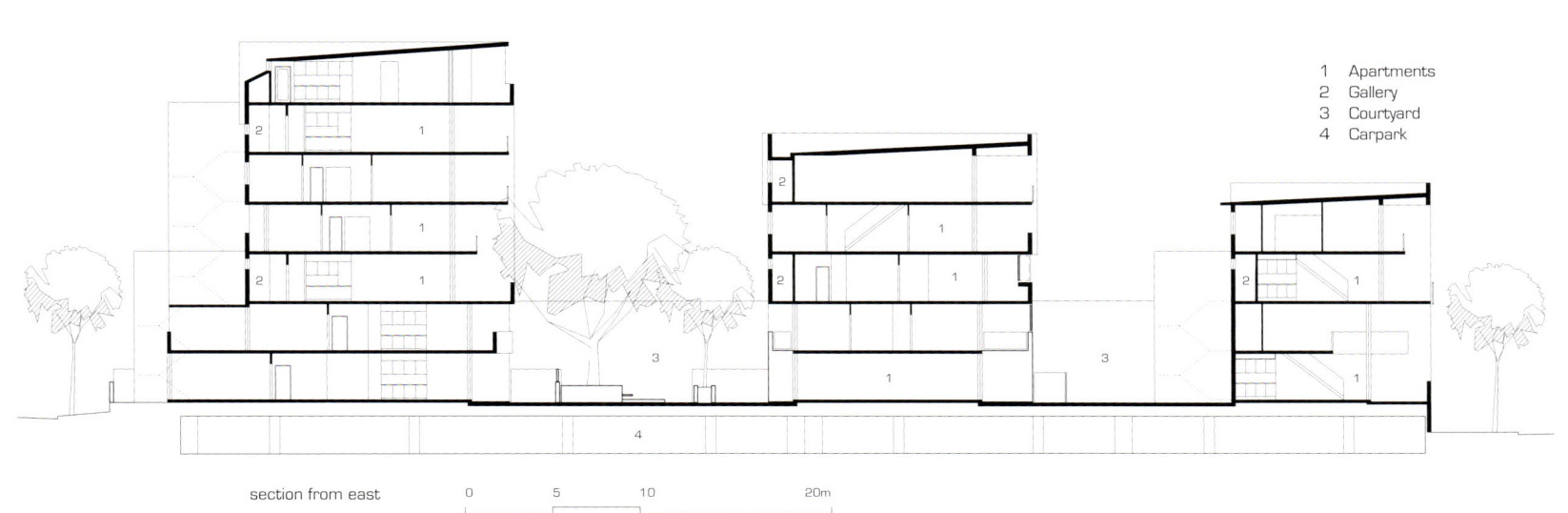

section from east   0   5   10   20m

1 Apartments
2 Gallery
3 Courtyard
4 Carpark

above : view of western block from north
left : view from southeast

1	Public Park
2	Through Site Link
3	Swimming Pool
4	Two Storey Lobbies
5	Access to Apartments Above
6	Gallery
7	Balcony
8	Living/Dining
9	Kitchen
10	Bedroom
11	Study
12	Bath
13	Ensuite

typical floor plan 0 5 10 20m

south elevation

left : courtyard from northeast
right : through-site link from south

Philip Drew

mondrian

Philip Drew is an eminent Sydney-based architect and critic. He studied architecture at the University of New South Wales and has a Masters degree from the University of Sydney

Article published in Architectural Review Australia 084, Winter 2003

Reacting against megastructures in T*he Architecture Of The Well-Tempered Environment*, published in 1969, Reyner Banham indicated that the next challenge facing architects would be to express the new mechanical and electrical environmental servicing technology. According to Banham, this would result in either "the final liberation of architecture from the ballast of structure, or its total subservience to the goals of mechanical service." Completed eight years later, the Pompidou Centre in Paris was a mixture of Achigram's 'Plug-in' aesthetic and megastructure; what Banham had failed to take into account in his calculation was the need to adopt a sustainable approach in architectural design. Rather than more and more economic growth, individuals looking to the future raised the prospect of achieving a sustainable society. At the time, Banham was fascinated by minimal shelter ideas, such as the invisible standard-of-living package within an inflatable bubble. Unfortunately, the projection of technological determinism did not result necessarily in some kind of ultimate liberated Hippydom, but its opposite, hyper-dependency on artificial systems.

The Mondrian apartments at Waterloo run counter to Banham's futuristic vision of services expressionism, and instead, flexible intensive servicing is dispensed in favour of a partially unplugged aesthetic of permeability. Transparency gives way to permeability: the absorption of structure by services gives way to naturally solar-conditioned arrangements. Structure has survived, but it is minimal and supports the aims of sustainable design. Gone is the aim of technological dematerialisation for its own sake and maker of scientific progress. In contrast to Banham's 'plug-in' inflated bubbles, Stanisic's living package is a permeable wafer for living, configured to maximise such green objectives as natural passive solar design. The model in this instance for architectural permeability is the car radiator: such a comparison would have delighted Banham, yet surprisingly, the outcome is one of limited transparency and pared down structure not greatly different visually from Banham's minimal plug-in shelter ideal. You could describe Mondrian as minimalism by another route.

It is the air flow over a car radiator's thin copper grille which cools circulating engine-water. To augment air flow, a thermostat-controlled electric fan is usually fixed behind the radiator, which operates when the vehicle is idling. Stanisic's Mondrian apartments resemble the car radiator insofar as it maximises frontal area, thus the area of the north façade is maximised to take advantage of the northerly aspect. Similarly, the apartment depth is kept to a minimum of 16 metres to exploit a five-degree centigrade temperature differential between the cold south across to the hot north façade. The anonymous crate-structure façade was achieved by using thin vertical precast concrete blade-walls and projecting horizontal concrete floors and balconies. The grain of the apartment façade is far coarser than that of a car radiator, but it has been softened by the presence of louvred aluminium privacy screens that break down the scale and add a measure of delicacy to the large glazed fronts. Frank Stanisic likes to explain that his Mondrian apartments are a case of green on white: green sustainable building principles imposed on a clean modernist aesthetic in concert with industrial prefabrication and standardisation techniques. This statement underlines his commitment to modern architectural principles and their alignment with green objectives. According to Stanisic, the ideal building footprint is a thin permeable wafer of apartments proportioned so that it maximises exterior surface area, rather than, as occurs in central-core towers, aiming to maximise floor area while minimising

Mondrian.

outside wall area regardless of orientation or view. Hence, the north exposure to maximise sunny exposure is combined with crossover planned apartments, which facilitate cross-ventilation and limit the frequency of access galleries to every second floor level across the southern backs. At 279 hectares, Green Square is the largest comprehensive redevelopment attempted in Sydney thus far. Housing developments such as Mondrian achieve housing densities five times greater than that of Paddington or Glebe.

The earliest inner suburbs around the Sydney CBD to be redeveloped – such as Paddington on the east side after 1965 and Darling Harbour, Ultimo and Glebe in the mid-1980s – all clung to the harbour edge. Waterloo was left till last, till 1998, since it lacks the natural advantages of harbour views and interesting filigree of points and coves. Its principal advantages are its proximity to the CBD and its flatness. But even its flatness is a liability since the area is subject to flooding. The natural landscape was erased in the 19th century and replaced by a mixture of tanning, woolwashing, brickworks, metalwork industries and Chinese market gardens. Unlike the harbour locations which exploited their proximity to the harbour, at Green Square it is the quality of the architecture and urban design that is crucial, whatever there is that is attractive has to be embedded in the developments: architects cannot sit back and let the landscape do it all. The result really is a test of architecture and imagination. Mondrian is less than five kilometres directly south of the Sydney CBD, off Elizabeth Street. It is less than 10 minutes walking distance from Green Square Station on the new Airport rail link. Lacking natural landscape assets and with no water views, the response has been to create environmental amenity. Augmenting the green finger courtyards that part the precise grey parallel blocks, a slab of aquamarine blue water in a raised swimming pool opposes at right angles the public access across the site. The development adopts a mixed strategy that emphasises sustainability, consistency of urban form with buildings that strengthen street edges and developments which look inwards and establish values within themselves. A real surprise is the presence of a series of parks in the master plan area: these were included in a formal structural armature and serve as a framework for accreting the new urban fabric in much the same way a sculptor uses an armature to support and build up a form. In a quite deliberate sense, the park armature is a substitute for Sydney Harbour, but its effect is very different. Whereas the harbour disrupts continuity of street patterns and forces roadways to deviate around it, at Green Square, the park necklace has a unifying effect that binds precinct together and increases its cohesion and identity. Associated with the park armature are the ideas of its extension as a series of interconnected natural courtyards within blocks supplementing and extending the principle of green areas, which are themselves enclosed within the hard-edged street framework, and of housing connecting to the external backbone of parks. Recent Swedish research has shown that parks do impact on the local microclimate, and a linked system – besides being aesthetically desirable – will also promote cooler conditions in their vicinity.

Mondrian has 137, one, two and three bedroom apartments in four slim blocks, stepping up in height from the north to the south and separated by individual east-west finger courtyards to give maximum sun. The building coverage is 38 percent, leaving the remainder of the 75.7 metre deep site for open space in the form of a pocket park on Powell Street, garden courts, communal courtyards and a public pedestrian access-way linking Powell Street with Short Street. The crossover arrangement of the two-storeyed apartments with access galleries on every second floor enables cross-ventilation by warm and temperate land-sea breezes, while making the buildings more efficient by reducing the area taken up by circulation. The one- and two-storeyed crate-structure has been manipulated to provide thirty different plan layouts across the range of one, two and three bedroom apartments. The architectural diversity was sought to give choice and avoid monotony with the hope that this will attract social diversity. The passive solar aspect of the apartments is straightforward and readily comprehended, but there are refinements that add considerably to the attractiveness of the apartments, such as the generous deep plantation spotted gum balconies, double-storey, light-filled lobbies, and operable and fixed sun control and shading. The deeply set back glazed north elevation is calculated to admit low-angle winter sun and to exclude high-angle summer sun. On the opposite south elevation, the windows are small. Most apartments have dual north and south orientations to increase sun penetration early and late in the day, and thin finger courtyards extend out from the public pedestrian cross-connection to separate the apartment blocks. Life-cycle assessment including embodied energy and maintenance were considered in choosing the materials: plantation spotted gum was used for the balcony decks, pool decks and court screens, and mainly concrete blocks and precast concrete panels cast off the site were used for external and party walls, having the advantage of reducing on-site waste and greater quality. Mondrian cost $26.5 million with a GFA rate of $2,200 per square metre, which is remarkably low compared to current domestic construction.

There are three main ideas in the Green Square Structural Master Plan: permeability, connectivity and interdependency. Permeability describes the quality of penetration, infiltration and overspread in the apartment blocks themselves, which suggests openness to natural processes such as the sun and movement of air through the interior spaces driven by convection. Connectivity is illustrated by the provision of public access across the site. With their tense constructions of primary colour elements on an empty field of white, Mondrian's abstractions are perfect demonstrations of plastic permeability. Also, with their intuitive references to spirituality and the construction of an inner-reality, they seem cut off from nature in any direct or recognisable way. Stanisic apartments are physically cut off from nature, from Sydney Harbour: hence their meaning as architecture is internal, whatever quality they contribute arises from the perfection of the architectural means employed, rather than by any allusions to nature. Both in Piet Mondrian's paintings and the apartment architecture, the quality of being permeable brings about an openness and 'throughness' to coin a word, which focuses on the inside of things.

Architecture around Sydney Harbour is noticeably complacent, it doesn't try very hard, mostly resting easy in the knowledge that whatever its shortcomings, the harbour will make up for the shortfall. When the environment is so wonderful, architecture does not have to do much. But, away from the harbour, the story is very different. More like the challenge of Melbourne. It is only in such exceptional instances as the Sydney Opera House, which amplify the *genius loci* of its harbour location poetically, do we encounter architecture which not only justifies but illuminates its setting. Work such as the Mondrian apartments illustrates how the stimulus of hard sites that ask more of the architect can be an advantage. In the absence of anything being there, the Mondrian apartments constructs its own meaning out of the dynamic interaction of physical and spatial permeability, and its connection with its new surroundings.

Alexandria 2001-2005

SPECTRUM

Spectrum, occupying three perimeter buildings of between three and six storeys, and containing 50 one to four bedroom apartments, represents another important shift in the oeuvre of Stanisic Associates. A medium density housing development that includes SOHO apartments, Spectrum's dominant frontage runs along the busy and very public McEvoy Street. Located on an irregular site wedged between McEvoy Street and Lawrence Street (to the west), this 'brown-fill' site, formed by the amalgamation of property acquisitions from an abandoned arterial road, was compressed between a series of industrial warehouse renovations and 19th century terrace houses. The project was therefore as much a restorative urban infill project as it was one of collective housing.

Into this context, the architects inserted a surprisingly accommodating series of buildings and open spaces: both public and private. All apartments achieve an extremely high level of environmental amenity, with north-facing living spaces, outdoor balconies, courtyards and atriums. At first glance, the McEvoy Street elevation denotes a highly abstract architecture: white, linear and rhythmic, which contrasts with the crimson blade walls that frame the apartments, the vivid orange lift lobbies, and a curtain wall that encloses the gallery circulation promenade. However, this abstraction and diagrammatic approach is one that, Frank Stanisic argues, supplies the requisite freedom and flexibility to negotiate such difficult sites. Providing a delightful 'frame' for living, this architecture does not signify program through nostalgic reference

courtyard from west

courtyard from northeast

to house or domesticity, but rather through the careful configuration and orientation of the individual apartments: spacious well-ventilated dwellings are denoted by screened outdoor spaces, and balconies with views to the central courtyard garden. Addressing the public character of McEvoy Street, and in response to changing demographics and demands for work arrangements, a series of SOHO apartments occupy the ground floor level, facilitating flexible 'live, work' arrangements. The six to fourteen metre setback for proposed road widening along McEvoy Street has been landscaped as a moat-like, grassed swale with pedestrian bridges.

With Spectrum's surprising malleability of form – non-formulaic and carefully orchestrated – each elevation makes a particular response to the adjacent streetscape, as well as to the specific environmental orientation. The south-facing McEvoy Street elevation is, as Stanisic states, "road architecture" – streamlined and robust, revealing his interest in the Russian Constructivists – whilst the Lawrence Street elevation is more domestic, with a scale broken down through the modular arrangement of balconies and screens. The north-facing façades, looking onto the enclosed communal garden courtyard, are different again: operable aluminium louvre screens form a kinetic veil to the structured crate-like character of the apartments and, in its operability, this elevation takes on a changeable sculptural aesthetic that the architects were to pursue further in later projects.

Spectrum is redolent with surprise and subtle contradiction: apartment flexibility is encouraged through internal sliding walls between bedrooms and living rooms, and in the southern block, facing McEvoy Street, lightness is achieved through the northern orientation of living spaces and balconies, and a crossover plan that creates natural ventilation. The other two apartment blocks have a Torrens Title terrace configuration, with deep private courtyards and deep balconies. The block facing Lawrence Street has the most difficult site position with an east-west orientation, and centrally placed atriums draw light into the living, kitchen and bathroom spaces. Spectrum, with its diversity of expression and accommodation types, and its efficient, economic construction and planning, is an example of what Stanisic describes as "climatically responsive modernism," which could also be phrased as 'eco-minimalism': a term with roots in early 20th century modernism and, in particular the *'Existenz Minimum'* of Germany's *'Neue Sachlichkeit'* (New Objectivity).

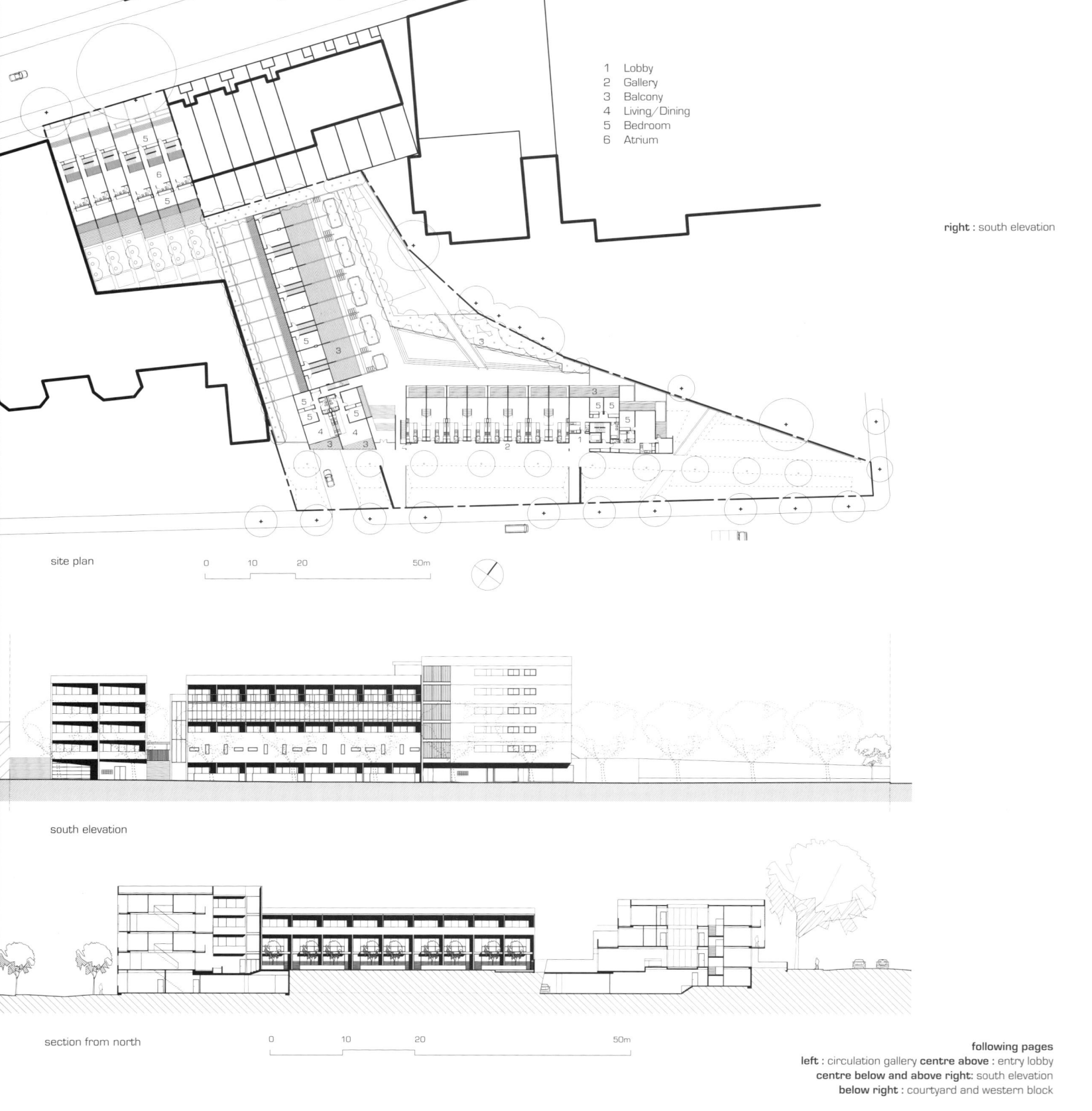

1 Lobby
2 Gallery
3 Balcony
4 Living/Dining
5 Bedroom
6 Atrium

site plan

0 10 20   50m

south elevation

section from north

0 10 20   50m

right: south elevation

following pages
left: circulation gallery **centre above**: entry lobby
centre below and above right: south elevation
below right: courtyard and western block

Alexandria 2001-2005

DATUM

Located on a long narrow corner site in Alexandria with a dominating southeast frontage to Euston Road, a northeast frontage to Maddox Street, and facing northwest to Euston Lane at the rear, Datum is situated on another difficult brown-fill site. Bounded by noisy roads, and a mix of industrial buildings and residential developments, Datum can be seen as a companion to Stanisic Associates' contemporaneous Spectrum project, adopting similar sectional, formal and material explorations. Spanning the length of its long, highly visible site, with tones of white and grey rendered concrete block overlaid with finely-detailed operable aluminium plantation louvred screens, Datum is an even more robust and uncompromising expression of what Frank Stanisic describes as "road architecture."

The horizontal linearity of the Euston Road façade constitutes an architecture of rhythmic layered abstractions, recalling the functional buildings of early 20th century European modernism. The building can be read as a long perimeter form in two sections: punctuated by vertical entry light-wells, and bookended by a corner block at the busy intersection of Euston Road and Maddox Street. This main building contains 44 two bedroom, one bedroom, and study terrace apartments, all of which span the width of the building to enable double orientation and cross-ventilation. Living areas and balconies face northwest, whilst the apartments in the corner building have northwest or northeast orientations, resulting in corner cross-ventilation. This attention to orientation and

southeast elevation

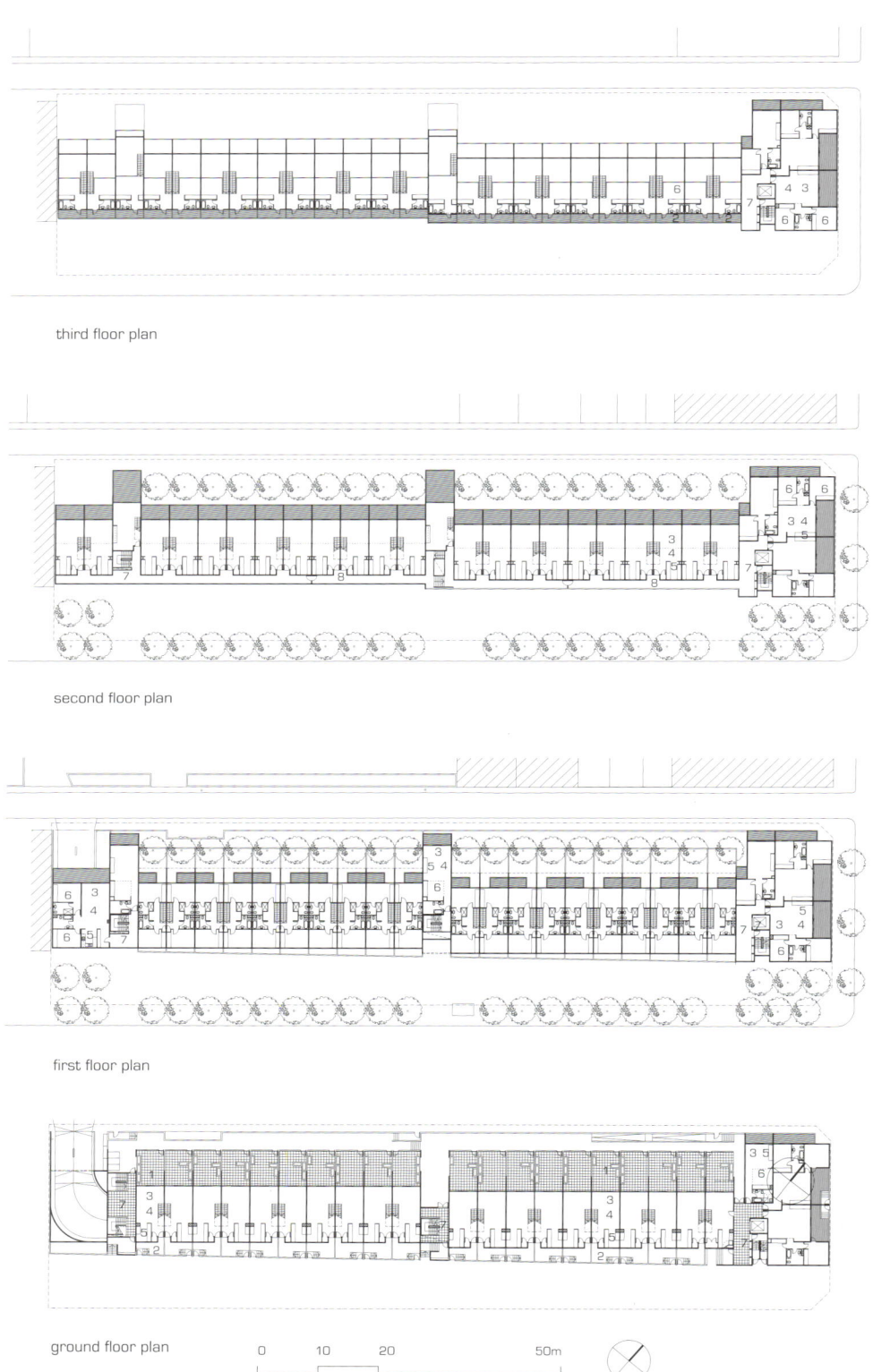

third floor plan

1 Court
2 Terrace
3 Living
4 Dining
5 Kitchen
6 Bedroom
7 Lobby
8 Gallery

second floor plan

first floor plan

ground floor plan 0 10 20 50m

right : circulation gallery
far right : entry light-well

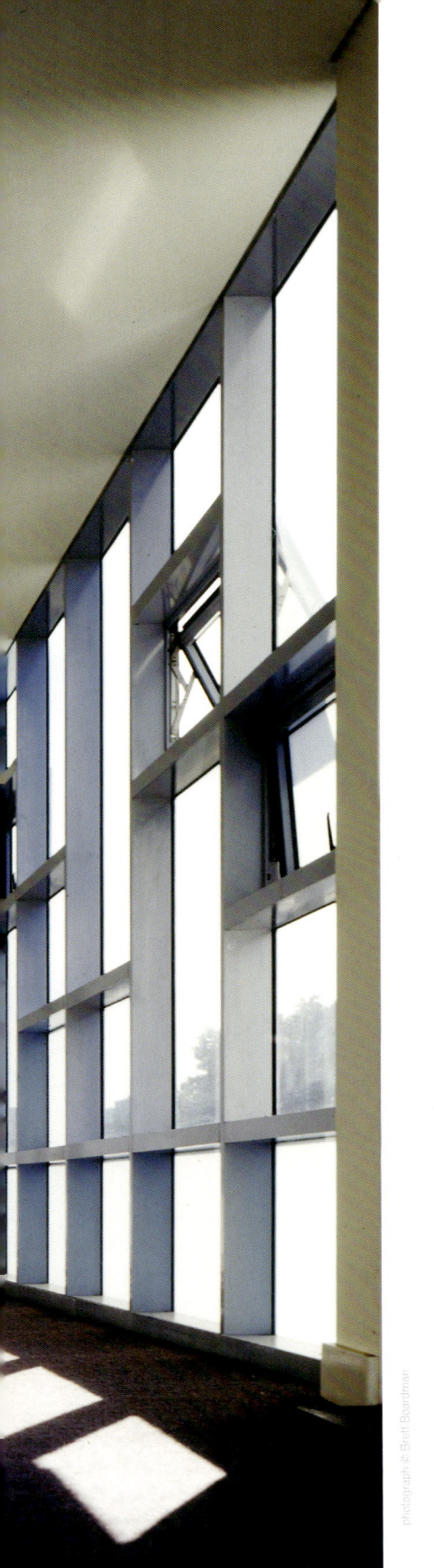

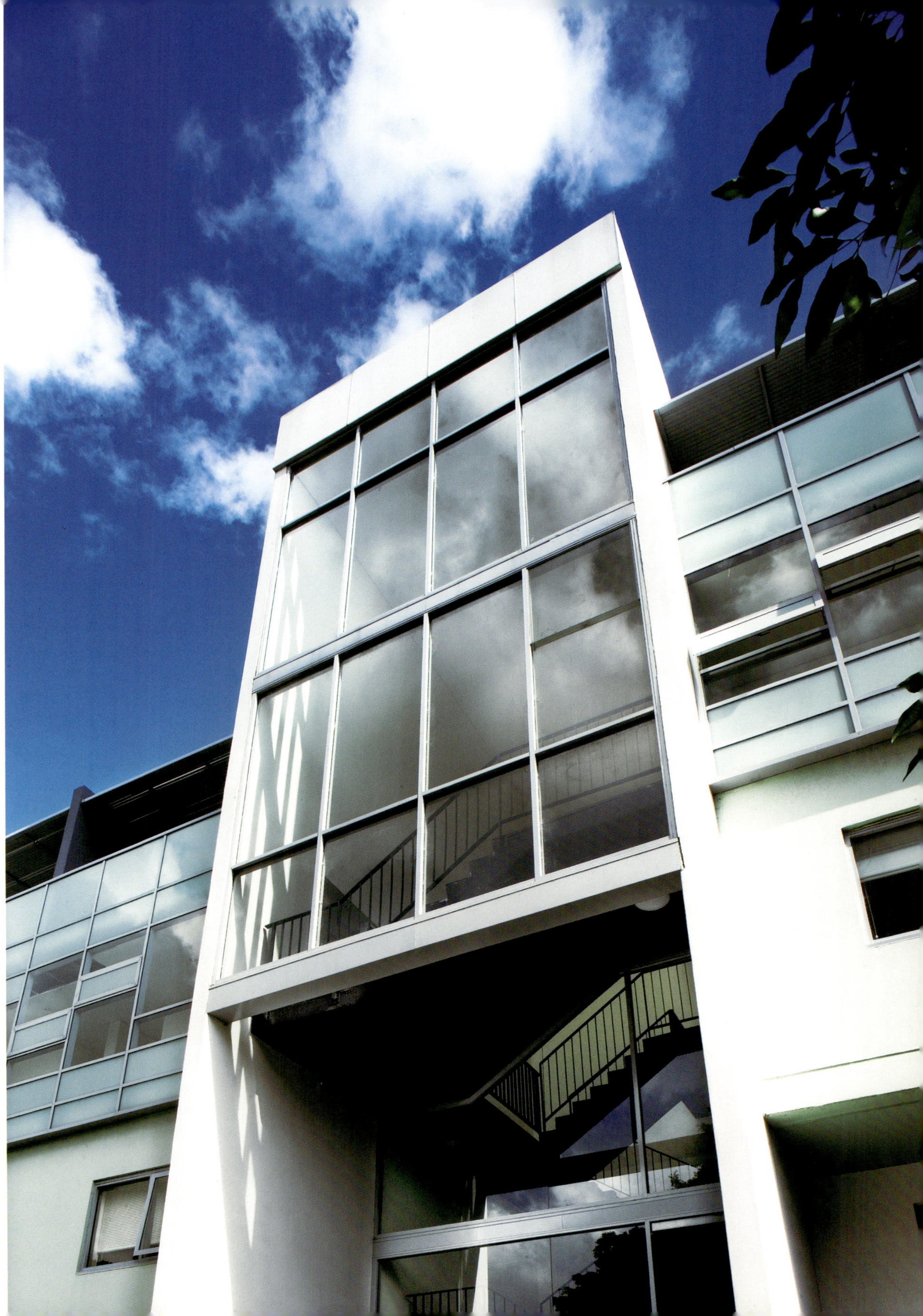

photograph © Brett Boardman

above and right : northwest elevation facing Euston Lane

materiality reduces the need for double glazing and air-conditioning, and along with the rooftop solar panels, and water management and collection strategies, Datum is another fine example of Stanisic Associates' 'Eco Minimalist' approach.

As with Spectrum, access to apartments is through light-filled lobbies, which lead up to enclosed access galleries with operable glazing. This gallery system, with transparent and opaque glazing panels, and expressed vertical mullions, animates the elevation and illuminates the street below at night, thus enlivening an otherwise severe streetscape. Viewed from Euston Road, this robust block with a solid base becomes progressively lighter and more transparent at the third and fourth levels, with open balconies and fixed metal sunhoods on the top storey. In contrast, the rear elevation, facing Euston Lane, has a vertical emphasis expressed by a cellular structure of attached terraces, interrupted by sky courtyards with broad projecting sun-screens at the upper levels. Continuing the building's tectonic expression of an abstraction detailed with an industrial or technological economy, aluminium louvres, screens and blinds are used for privacy and for protection from the afternoon sun. Unlike its precedents, driven by a more aesthetic determinism, the modern abstract language of Datum works to achieve the overarching ambitions of creating a contextually responsive urban project: an environmentally and socially responsive complex of light-filled, cross-ventilated, spacious dwellings.

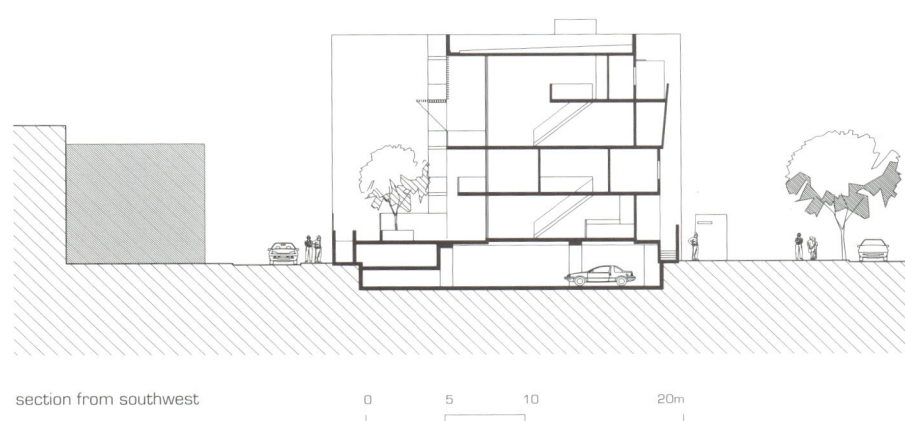

section from southwest   0   5   10   20m

following pages
left : circulation gallery **centre above and centre below**
right : southeast elevation **centre below left and**
below right : northwest elevation **above right** : entry stairway

Photograph © Brett Boardman

Alexandria 2002-2009

222

Occupying a large irregularly shaped site, with two existing substantial developments on its northeast and southwest corners, 222 is one of Stanisic Associates' first large scale projects that explores mixed-use typology. A central location in Alexandria, with frontages to Botany Road, McEvoy Street and Wyndham Street, and to Retreat Street at the rear, necessitated an architectural response that worked 'in the round' to promote public connection and amenity. 222 reconciles the contextual differences between the three Hudson apartment buildings on the block and the adjacent smaller scale historical fabric of hotels, terrace houses, and the temple of the Yiu Ming Chinese precinct, whilst also serving as a gateway project at the intersection of Botany Road and McEvoy Street. It forms part of the Green Square Structural Masterplan, with an emphasis on 'architectural quality' and 'enhanced environmentally responsive residential amenity'.

The design *parti* comprised a fragmented block of edge buildings, which define a multi-level central courtyard with through-site public access. These buildings – varying in height from nine storeys at the Botany Road and McEvoy Street corner to four storeys along Retreat Street, adjacent to the Yiu Ming Temple – provide a measured scalar response to context, whilst establishing a highly robust architectural character. Green rendered concrete and linear expressive forms give way to an unfinished precast concrete: the elevations are a layered demonstration of concrete's expressiveness, contrasting with double-height sliding aluminium plantation shutters. For the glazed

east elevation

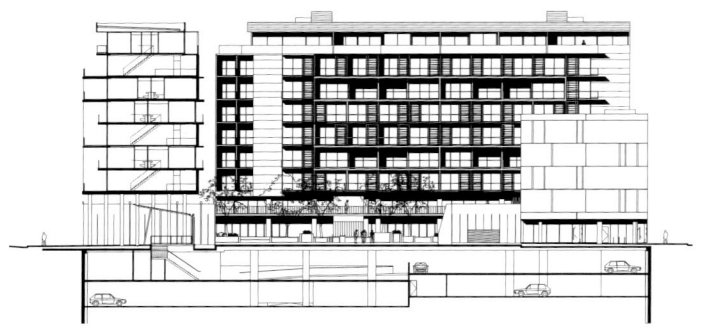
section from west

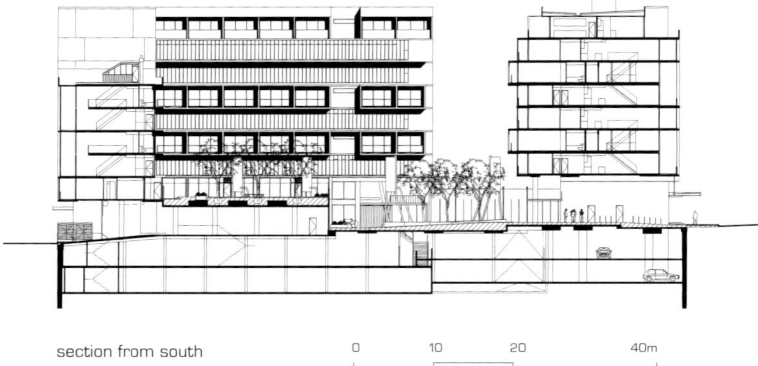
section from south

0 10 20 40m

access galleries and lift lobbies, the architects introduced slim panes of green, translucent and clear glazing, held between expressed mullions.

As with all Stanisic Associates projects, the detailing and articulation of elevations are intrinsically tied to the contextual and environmental conditions of each frontage's orientation, but as there are eight differing elevations, the result is highly dynamic and appropriate. The distinctive structured character of the *brise soleil* – gridded formations of apartments with deep balconies on the northern elevation – contrasts with the east and west elevations facing Botany Road and Wyndham Street, which are somewhat more plastic. The apartments press forward and are veiled by the plantation shutters, whilst the patterned glazing of lift lobbies interrupts that ordering and, on the McEvoy Street elevation, rise up and above the top-level apartments. Bookending the elevations, the simpler planar surfaces of the corner points indicate a shift in orientation.

122 apartments, of between one to three bedrooms, and of one or two storeys, accommodate a variety of demographics and lifestyles, whilst 2000 square metres of retail space is placed at ground level along Botany Road and McEvoy Street. Whilst not all apartments have northern orientation due to the site restrictions, they receive sunlight at some time during the day, and environmental responsiveness is achieved with balconies or courtyards attached to living areas.

Continuing Frank Stanisic's interest in modernism, and particular those modernists with a strong social and urban agenda, references can be detected to the Brutalist movement of the 1960s and 70s, and in particular to Le Corbusier's early Brutalist explorations of the late 1950s and 60s, such as the expressive concrete buildings at Chandigarh, India, 1951-64, at Cambridge, USA, 1961-64, and the Monastery of La Tourette, France, 1953-57. As with these Corbusian examples, and in its juxtaposition of rhythms and sequences of glazing, openings, and structure, 222 possesses a certain musicality: it is perhaps less of an example of Stanisic's 'Eco Minimalism' than one of 'Eco Brutalism'.

façade overlooking courtyard

left: east elevation **above**: southern block from courtyard
above right: eastern block from courtyard **below right**: courtyard from north

northern block from courtyard

second floor plan

third floor plan

ground floor plan

1	Lobby	7	Balcony
2	Gallery	8	Entry
3	Corridor	9	Retail
4	Living/Dining	10	Courtyard
5	Bedroom	11	Public Way
6	Terrace	12	Loading

first floor plan

above left: circulation gallery **above centre and below**: typical apartment interiors **right**: northern block from courtyard

Roseberry 2002-2008

CODA

Sydney's architecture is typically characterised by buildings set in sundrenched waterside locations, with minimal white forms aimed at the view and at 'domesticating' the view. The view dominates, and the architecture doesn't need do very much other than provide an inhabitable frame. So when there is no view, the site is 'brownfill' post-industrial, and the brief is for collective housing, the demands on the architect are far greater: the architecture is no longer secondary and it must perform across a number of levels. As Frank Stanisic says, "the potential for architecture is, in fact, greater on these sites, as the building must take on a presence and develop an interface with the street." The collective housing market is one dominated by developers and builders, and this territory, says Stanisic "is well and truly occupied." Within these highly competitive environments, however, innovation emerges, and Coda, located at the southern edge of Green Square in Rosebery, is an excellent example of architecture adding value to a site through an innovative design response.

The site, with a very 'busy' northern frontage curving at the eastern end as it follows the sweep of a disused tramline, is in a precinct undergoing urban renewal and is therefore in state of transition. The project called for architecture that would have a strong urban presence – an 'urban marker' – and activate the street, whilst providing a comprehensive environmental solution. Coda, with its distinctive carriage form 'skinned' by a metallic environmental screen, and with a floating roof sweeping across the top level of

north elevation

north elevation

two- and three-storey terrace apartments, has a notably expressive tectonic presence. The architects used the perimeter edge block to create an urban edge, which bends at the eastern corner in response to the site's geometries, with the seven-storey elevation organised horizontally. Raised on *piloti*, the apartment block is cantilevered above ground level, and in doing so, defines a glazed urban terrace with shops, a café and a restaurant that provide visual continuity through the site.

The slender building form, with a slim 'glass-to-glass' width of ten metres, becomes a permeable wall enclosing a communal sun-shaded courtyard. The apartment types, all two-storey and adopting the crossover plan, include one bedroom lofts, two bedroom terraces and three bedroom sky terraces. Organised in a spatial honeycomb structure, each apartment possesses double orientation, cross-ventilation, and north-facing living spaces. The building's skin, which Stanisic calls the 'environmental screen', is particularly sophisticated: this 'screen' – actually a three metre deep section – comprises metal framed double-height plantation shutters, multi-folding panels, and timber decked double-height 'sunroom' balconies accessed by sliding doors and louvred windows. This expanded threshold allows the apartments to breathe, and creates inviting, warm, light-filled living spaces. From Epsom Road, the *brise-soleil* of the environmental screen reads as a perforated shimmering skin: a jacket that wraps the building's elongated curving form. The sectional arrangement of crossover planning, with open access galleries placed at every second level, is clearly evident on the southern elevation. At each entry point on the access galleries, the entrance is widened and defined with white river stones to create a sense of arrival and a cue for the occupants to take over and modify as they wish.

Apartments are larger on the sixth and seventh storeys, containing two or three bedrooms, and seven of these apartments have extensive outdoor terraces, which extend the full length of the apartment. In these types, entry is directly into the terrace, with the living areas off to the sides. In an unprecedented move for relatively inexpensive apartments, the outdoor and indoor spaces are of equal size, creating environmentally comfortable and spatially dynamic apartments. Colour has been carefully orchestrated throughout, as the architects implemented a tempered sequence of arrival. From the street, movement is through darkly coloured access corridors into the apartments, which depending on their size and configuration, are white with dark warm greys for flooring, whilst the interior palette in the larger apartments comprises rich tones of brown and purple, with almost black ceilings. As Stanisic observes, white does not work inside these larger apartments and does not suit the overwhelming vivid intensity of Sydney's bright summer days. With Coda, the architects have produced a visually dynamic response to an impoverished urban context with an apartment block that houses a tempered, well-modulated environment, based on passive design principles and connection between interior and exterior.

east elevation

1 Courtyard
2 Retail Terrace
3 Retail
4 Lobby
5 Open Gallery
6 Living/Dining
7 Bedroom
8 Loggia
9 Sky Terrace
10 Balcony

sixth floor plan

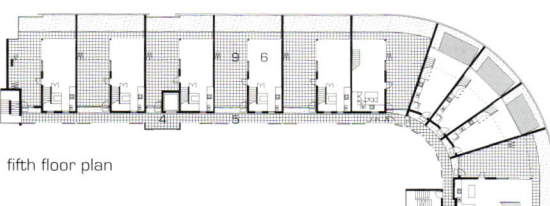

fifth floor plan

second and fourth floor plan

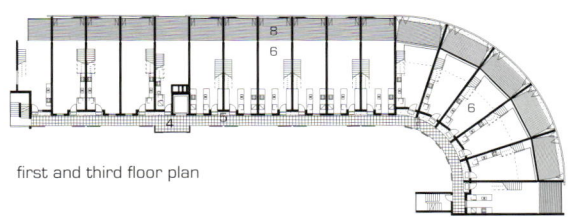

first and third floor plan

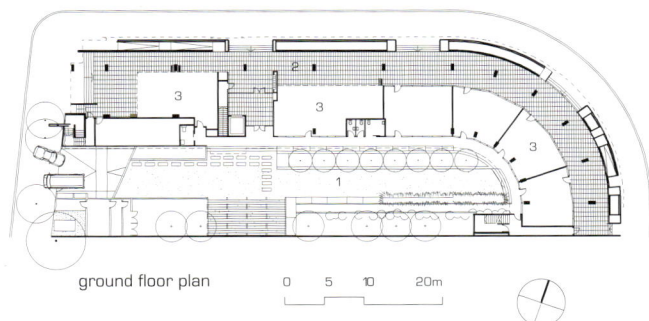

ground floor plan

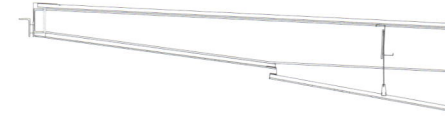

left : fifth floor sky terrace
below : southern access galleries

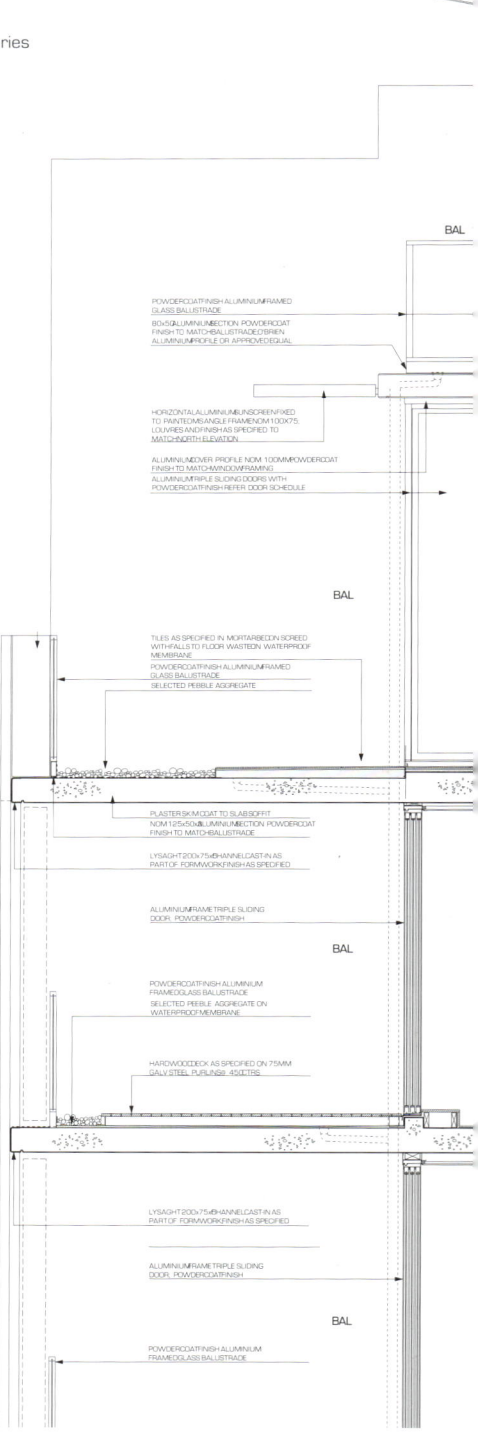

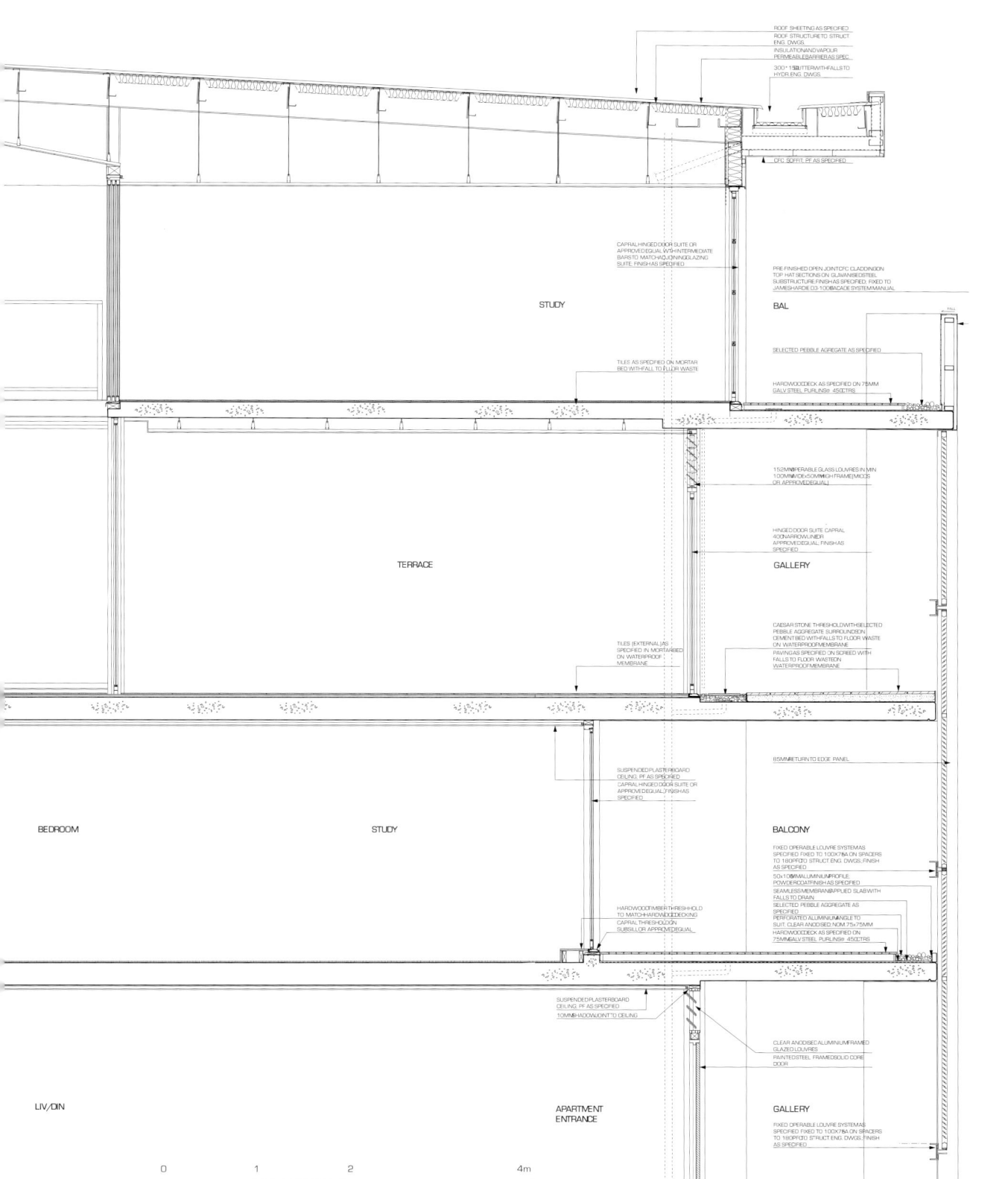

sky terrace section

above : view from courtyard **centre** : courtyard from west **right** : courtyard from southeast

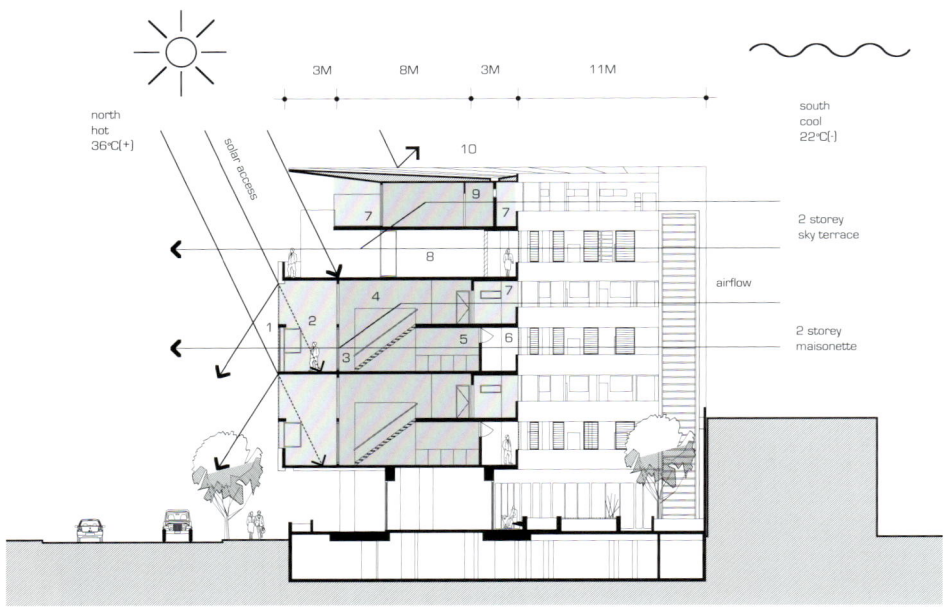

summer solstice

1 Sliding + Fixed Louvre Panels
2 Winter Garden
3 Sliding Doors
4 Living Area
5 Awning Window
6 Open Access Gallery
7 Balcony
8 Sky Terrace
9 Insulation
10 Roof

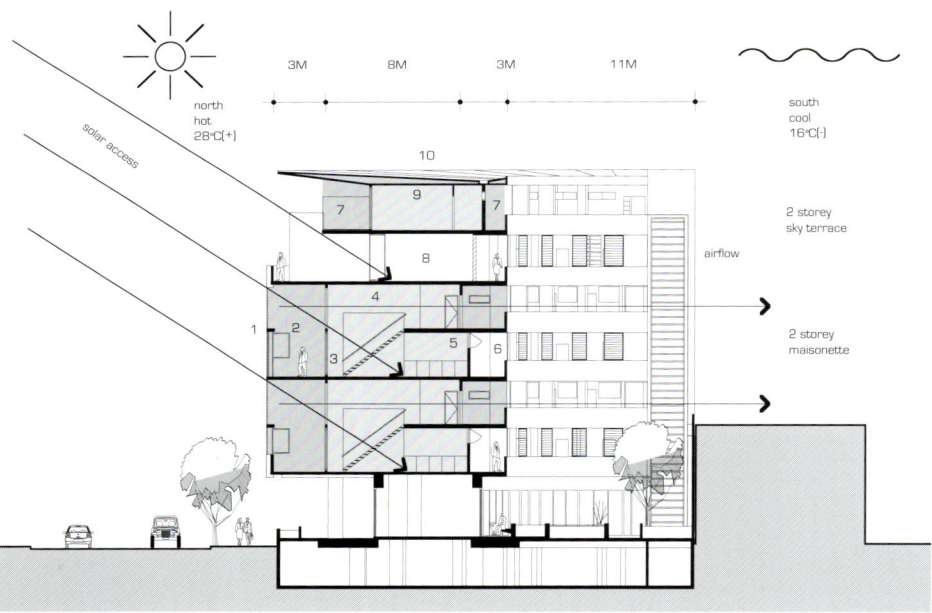

winter solstice

right: double-height apartment

following pages
below left: ground floor entry **all**
other images: apartment interiors

north elevation

Tarsha Finney

coda

Tarsha Finney is an architect, urbanist and senior lecturer in the School of Architecture at the University of Technology Sydney.

Article published in Monument August/September 2009

Architecture is all about 'the appropriation of occupied territory' argues Frank Stanisic, quoting Wolf Prix of Coop Himmelb(l)au. Between the developer, the council, the builder and the market, it's often hard to see where spatial innovation lies in the production of multi-residential or collective housing; but Stanisic, architect of the new 44 apartment project, Coda, in Sydney's inner south, argues that it's in the occupation of this already tightly held territory that the real work of architectural creativity and innovation lies. Coda, completed in 2008, is embedded on a trajectory of spatial experimentation into multi-residential housing that has been undertaken by the practice over the past 10 years. Through projects such as EDO (2007), Zone (2005) and Mondrian (2002), it is possible to see that the idea of sectional variation within the single dwelling, and the consequences of this for the collective block, is primary to the design research agenda of the practice. With Coda, Stanisic takes one of the seminal spatial innovations of the 20th century, the double storey crossover apartment popularised by Le Corbusier in his Unité d'Habitation in Marseille (1946-1952), and pushes it in another direction: further away from the single level and spatially dull residential 'flat' that dominates apartment provision in our cities.

Coda sits in a neighbourhood in transition. Surrounded by used car lots and mid-20th century light and heavy industrial warehouses, it is the first and smallest of three stages proposed for a site that forms part of the urban renewal program unfolding around Green Square. Made up of ground, main body and floating roof terrace, Coda is classical in form: in the sense that Modernism is all about the displacement of classical concepts if we follow Alan Colquhoun. Stanisic deploys the block to ameliorate the noise from the busy intersection around which it wraps, creating a quiet communal courtyard space to the rear. Like the Unité, Coda is lifted up off the ground. Instead of an open plaza, however, the resulting space is glazed front and back, and fitted out for cafés, restaurants and a convenience store, with glazing that allows for a visual connection in either direction. Not so remarkable from the busy street, but from the quiet of the courtyard, the acoustic edge is taken off the traffic by the glazing, while colour and movement still filters thought unobtrusively.

The double-height roof space under a wide overhanging eave is reserved for larger three bedroom Sky Terrace apartments, while the main body of the building contains one and two bedroom apartments. It's here that Stanisic and his team begin to experiment with the section. In Coda, Le Corbusier's classic crossover apartment section from the Unité is halved vertically along one side of the access corridor. The now narrow block is perfectly suited to a Sydney specific climate and the demand for cross-ventilation. The access corridor is open to the south, which, like the Corbusian prototype, is placed at every second floor. The one and two bedroom apartments that lead off this are in part double-height as they fold back over the corridor, resulting in a kind of "sectional honeycomb," as Stanisic likes to say. The apartments are modestly finished with robust, generous double-height living spaces, and sun-drenched and malleable north-facing winter gardens that become verandas when the louvred façade is opened. Like the Unité, Coda aspires to community. In the access corridor, for example, the entry areas to each apartment are widened and set back, demanding appropriation by the users of the block in small gestures of individual identity that come in the form of plants and stone objects, markers framed thought the collective spatial experience. Objects indicative of the appropriation of another kind of territory.

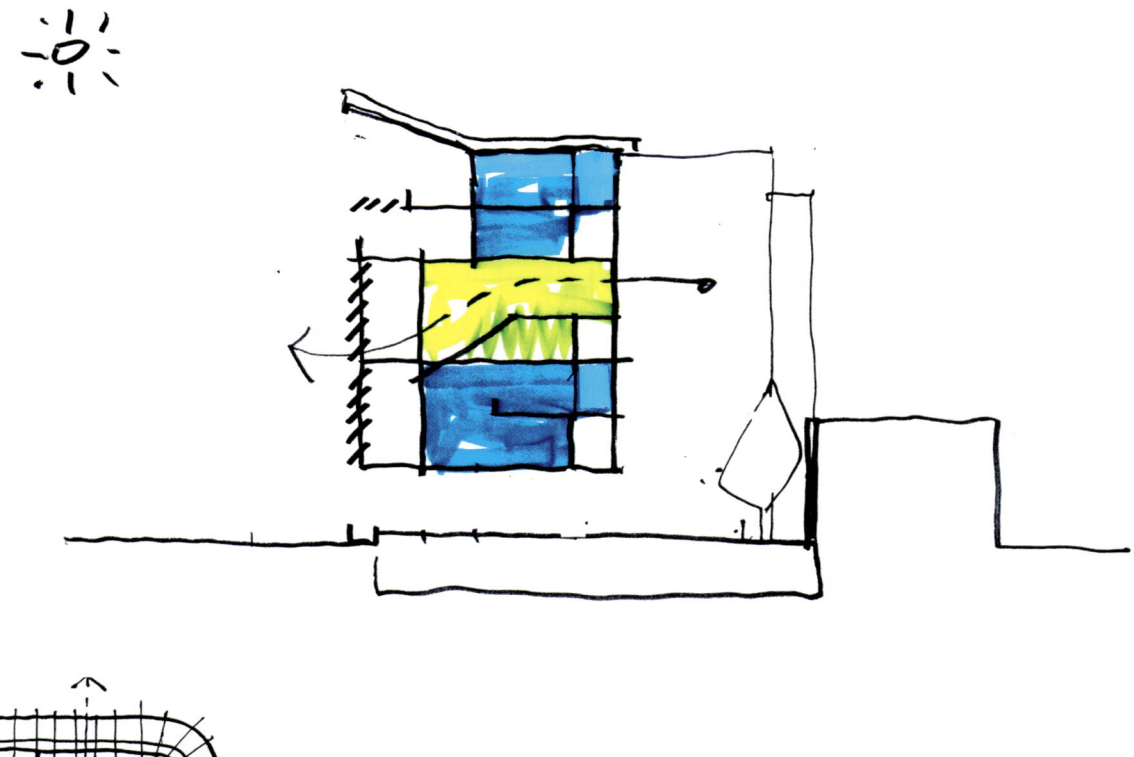

Burwood 2003 (unbuilt)

ELSIE

Located in the commercial centre of Burwood, in Sydney's inner-west, this proposal for a state-of-the-art working environment comprises approximately 16,600 square metres of floor space dispersed over seven levels, and includes a ground level café, a restaurant, a loading dock, and a three level underground car park. Whilst the appearance of the building is modern, with strong clean volumes and lines, simple planes, and transparent materials, the urban form is a response to the context with a diverse mix of offices, shops and residential buildings. The building height mediates a variety of adjacent two- and eight-storey buildings, and assuming an urban and public role, the design aims to define the adjoining streets and public spaces. Set back 21 metres from its northern street boundary and aligning with the northern face of the neighbouring office building, the building creates a sun-filled publicly accessible forecourt adjoining one of the car park portal entrances. The southern end is set back only nine metres from the street, aligned with the façade of the adjoining office building, and the form is brought down to two storeys, which engages the scale of the adjoining terraces and continues the two-storey street wall. The western elevation adjoins four-storey residential blocks and townhouses, and is divided by a vertical atrium and balconies, which establish a fragmented and smaller-scaled form, in keeping with the rhythm and scale of the adjoining buildings.

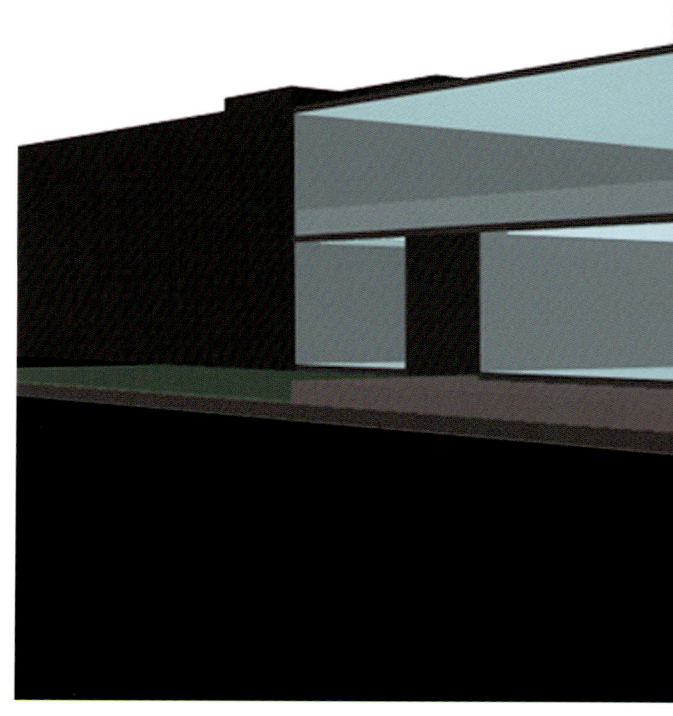

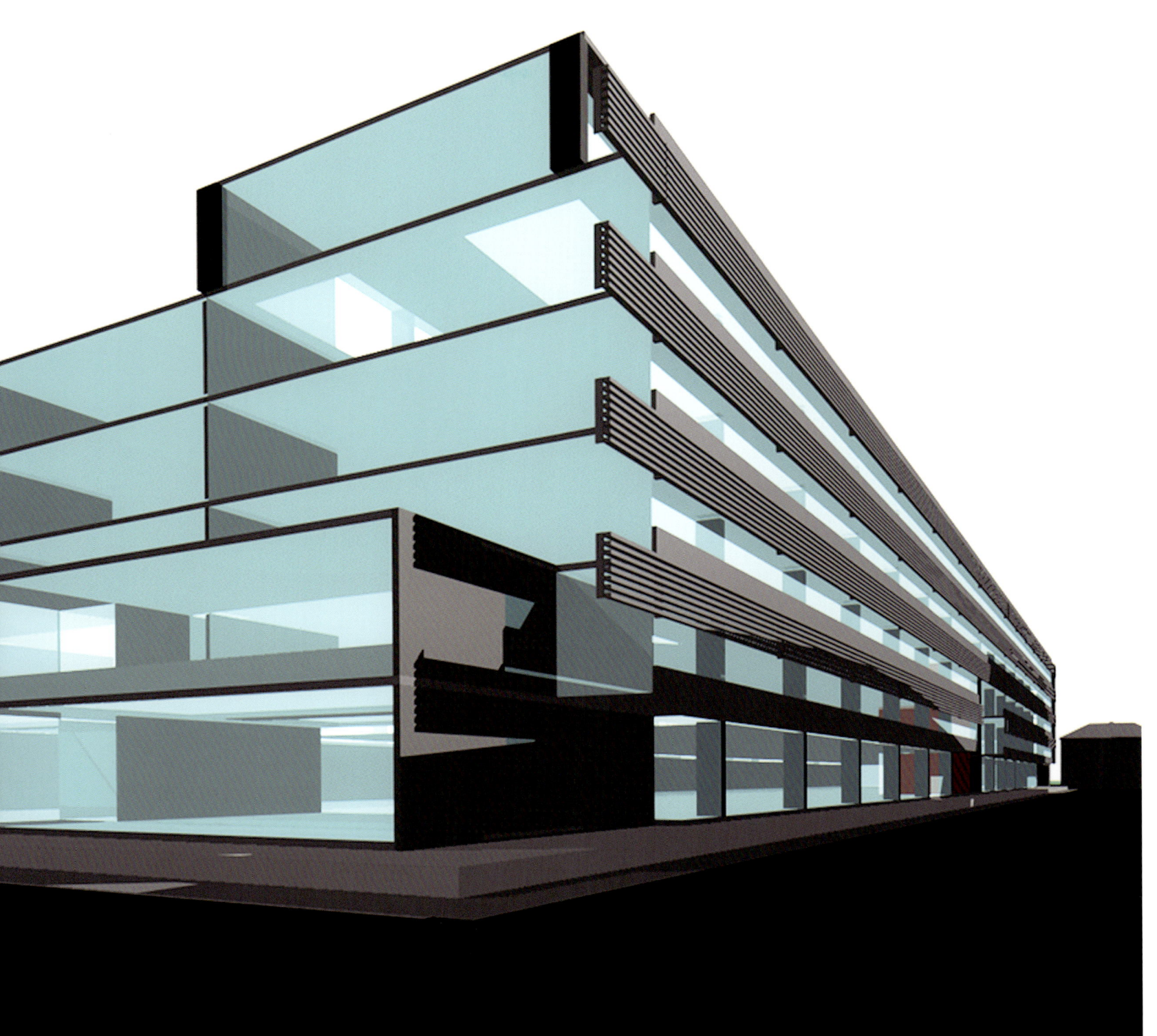

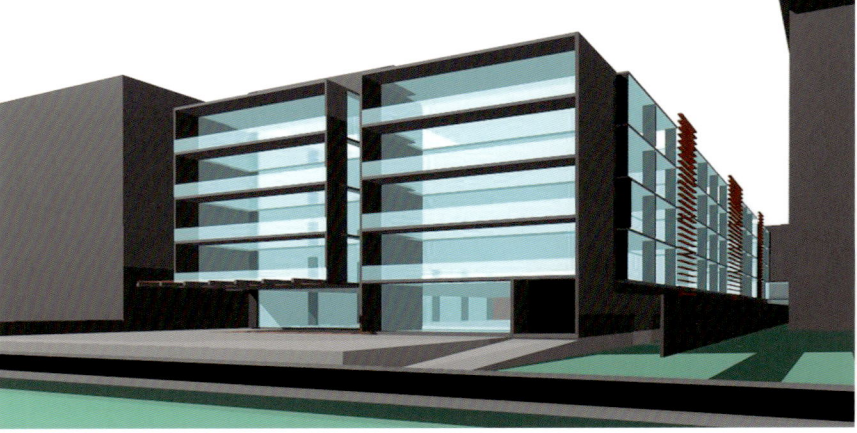
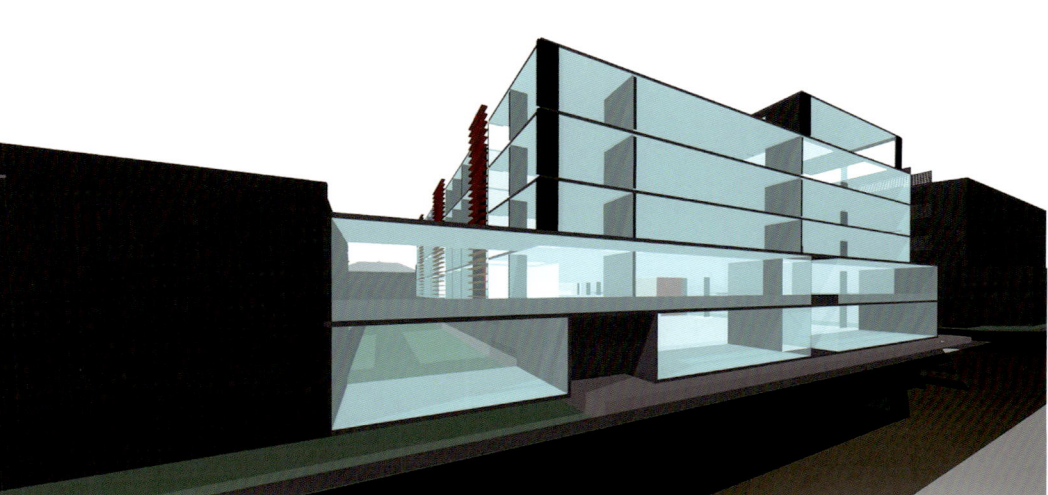

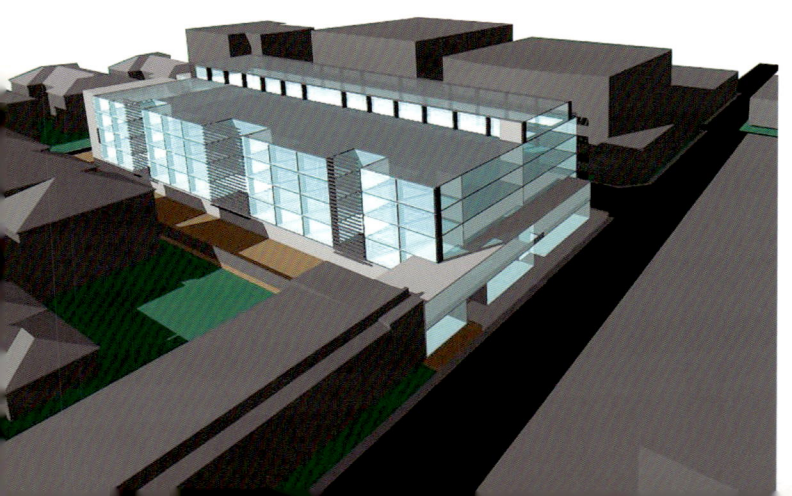
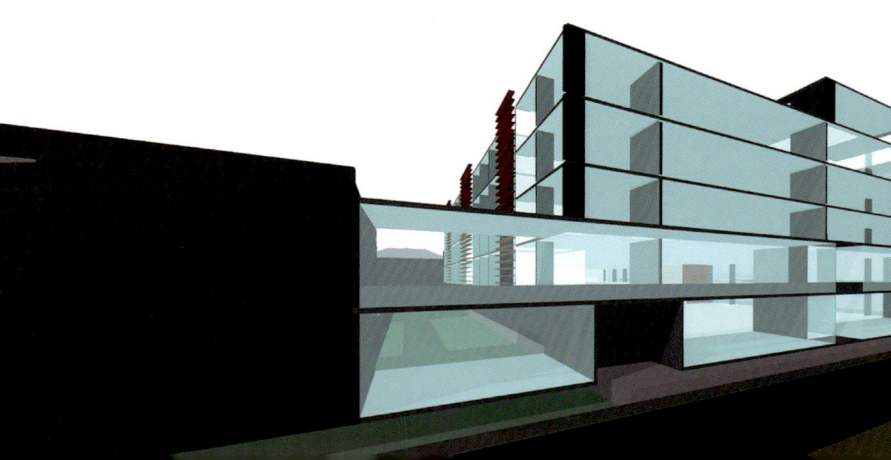

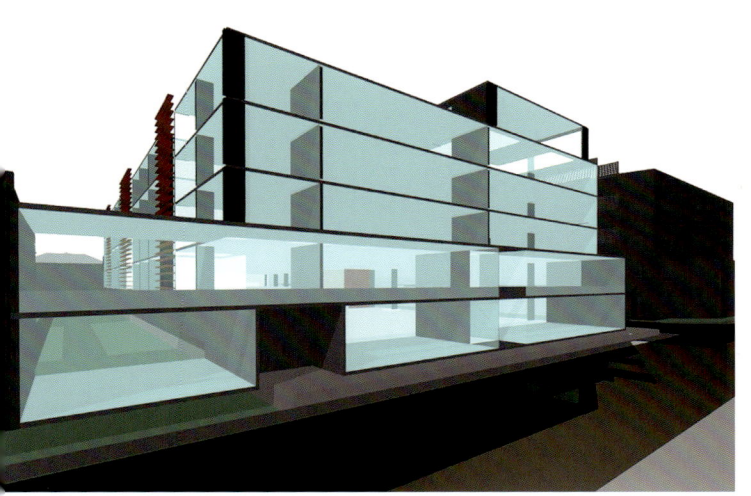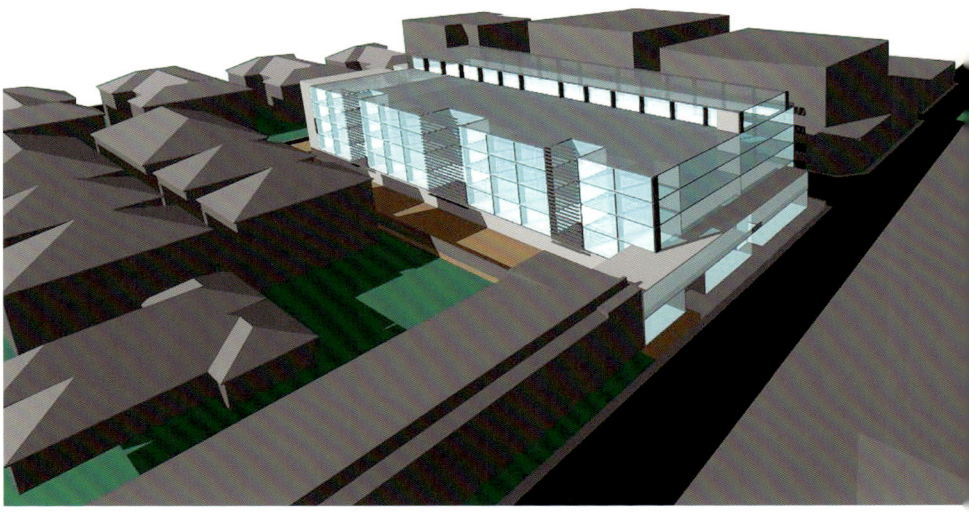

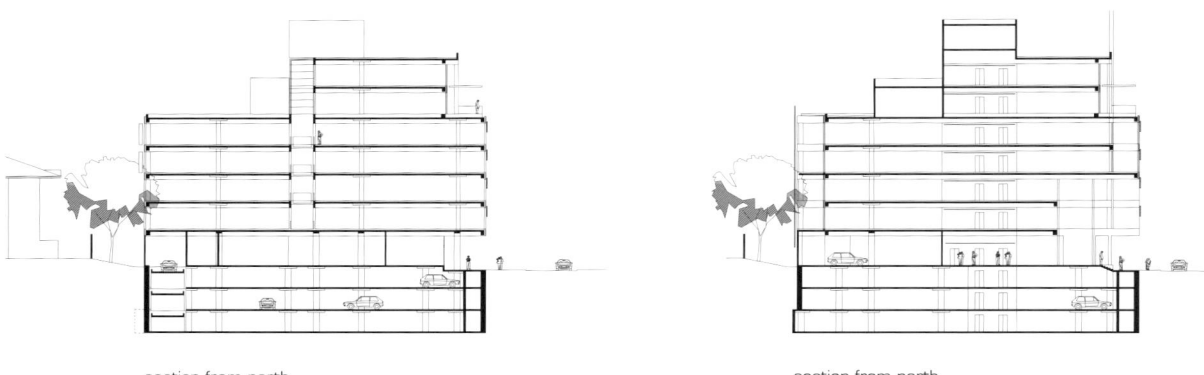

section from north   section from north

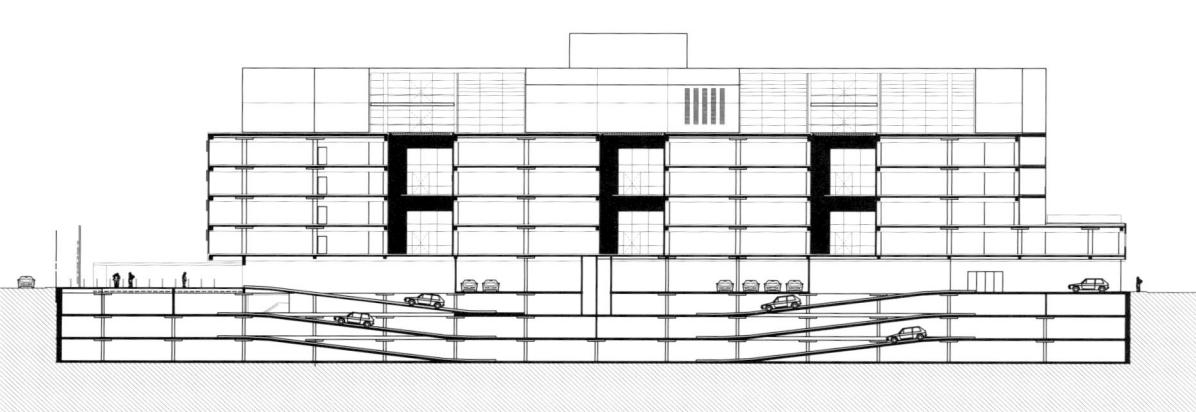

section from west

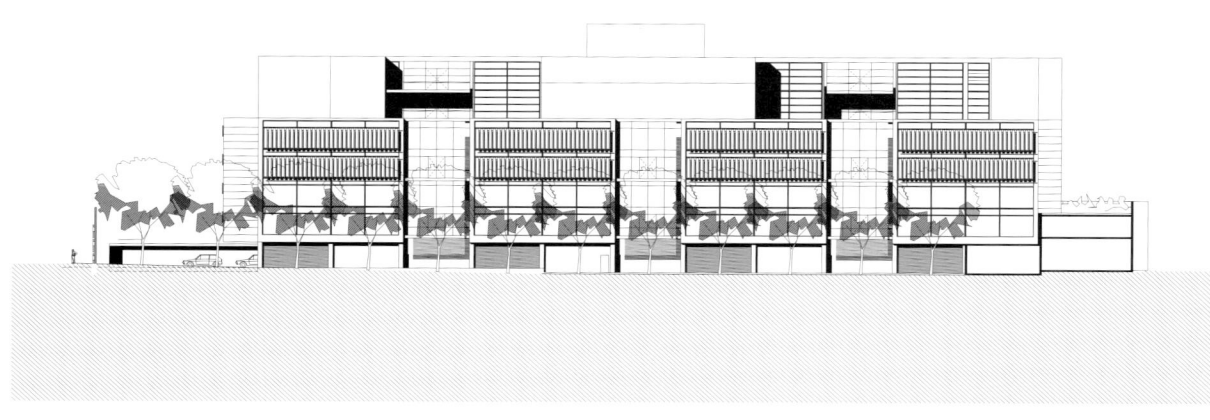

west elevation   0   10   20   40m

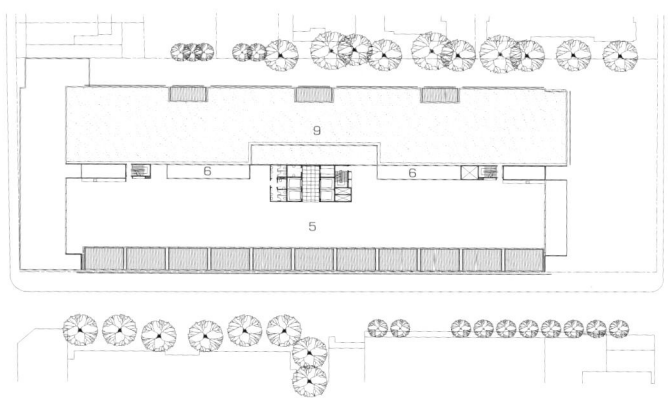

sixth floor plan

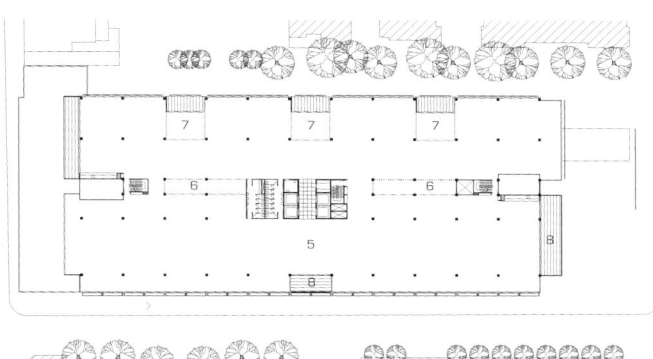

third floor plan

1 Public Forecourt
2 Cafe
3 Entry
4 Retail
5 Offices
6 Light and air well
7 Atria
8 Balcony
9 Terrace

Articulated as two linear bands, which adjust to the scale of their context, the buildings maximise north- and east-facing orientation whilst retaining privacy and solar access for their neighbours. Between the two building forms, a series of central light-wells bring natural light and ventilation into the office environments, and efficiently reduce what would have been 35 metre wide floor plans to 16 metre wide spaces. Open-air 'break-out' spaces are provided for staff, and take the form of perimeter atria and timber-decked balconies at each level, whilst expansive roof terraces at the upper levels provide larger, more public, outdoor areas. Providing a finer layer of detail to the planar elevations, a series of sun-shading metal screens, aluminium sunhoods and overhangs are applied to the north, east and west façades. As with all projects by Stanisic Associates, this attention to passive solar design and orientation creates an environmentally responsive building that minimises solar heat gain, and the need for air-conditioning or heating. As Frank Stanisic states, "The building has an intentionally direct, mechanistic appearance," which has evolved specifically from environmental performance criteria, rather than "preconceived picturesque images."

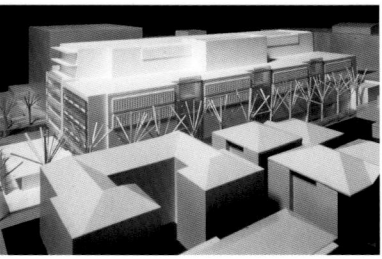

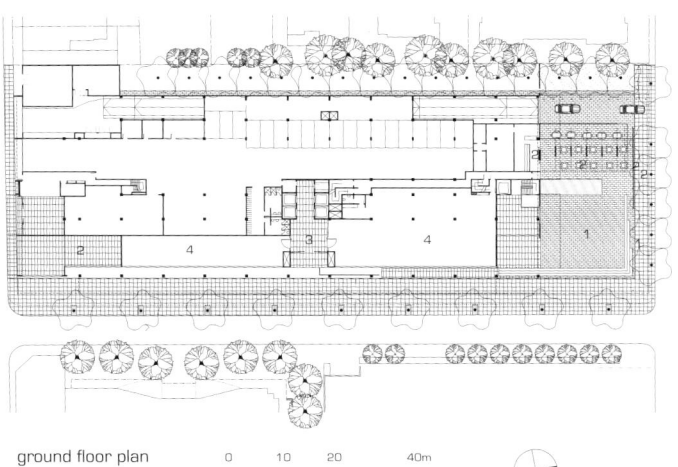

ground floor plan

Rhodes 2003 (unbuilt)

WATERSIDE (form)MATRIX

(form)Matrix is an exposition of a residential project that began as a competition-winning proposal for a site at Rhodes Waterside on the eastern shores of Homebush Bay. Adjacent to the Sydney Olympic site, the Rhodes peninsula has undergone extensive remediation and reclamation, and is intended to become an integral part of a proposed public and infrastructure network. The site possesses a threshold condition: one side looks west over the mangroves of Homebush Bay, whilst the other frontages interface with the public spaces of streets and park. With a long, curving solid street-edge building facing Shoreline Drive, connected to lighter finger buildings and courtyards overlooking Homebush Bay, the proposal by Stanisic Associates was conceived of as an abstracted, yet responsive, building that addressed the site's dual aspect. The site, which initially contained a five finger scheme comprising 150 apartments of varying bedroom size and configurations dispersed across the four- and six-storey buildings, was subsequently decreased in area and reduced to a three finger proposal by the developer.

Nevertheless, as with many Stanisic Associates' projects, (form)Matrix promoted experimentations and the testing of ideas and form, and the architects explored several key themes that found expression in later projects. One of two central ideas that drove the design was an exploration of a diversity of living environments contained within monumental, clearly delineated building forms, which questioned the degree to which a building's exterior can articulate its programmatic diversity

116 | 117

and variability. The other dominant idea resulted from the need to reconcile the robust and muscular presence of the curving 'urban street wall' building with the lighter pavilion buildings and their landscaped courtyards.

Reviving what Frank Stanisic describes as the "unresolved modernist theme of a machine for living," the tectonics reveal a strategy of reduction rather than addition, and restraint rather than overload, thus avoiding what he describes as the "fruit salad bowl" approach for collective housing where exteriors become overworked and repellent anti-urban objects. Based on a configuration of vertical and horizontal openings that express and reflect the varying degrees of sunlight penetration and the surrounding views, the contemporary language of the exterior of the buildings demonstrates a departure from the crate-like cellular expression found in previous Stanisic projects. The planning creates an unexpected diversity, as the curving street wall is arranged internally around what the architects describe as a '(form)Matrix': a patchwork system of interlocking, one-and two-storey types, with studio, one, two and three bedroom units structured within a unique 'triple crossover' arrangement in plan, section and elevation that forms part of a reiterated module.

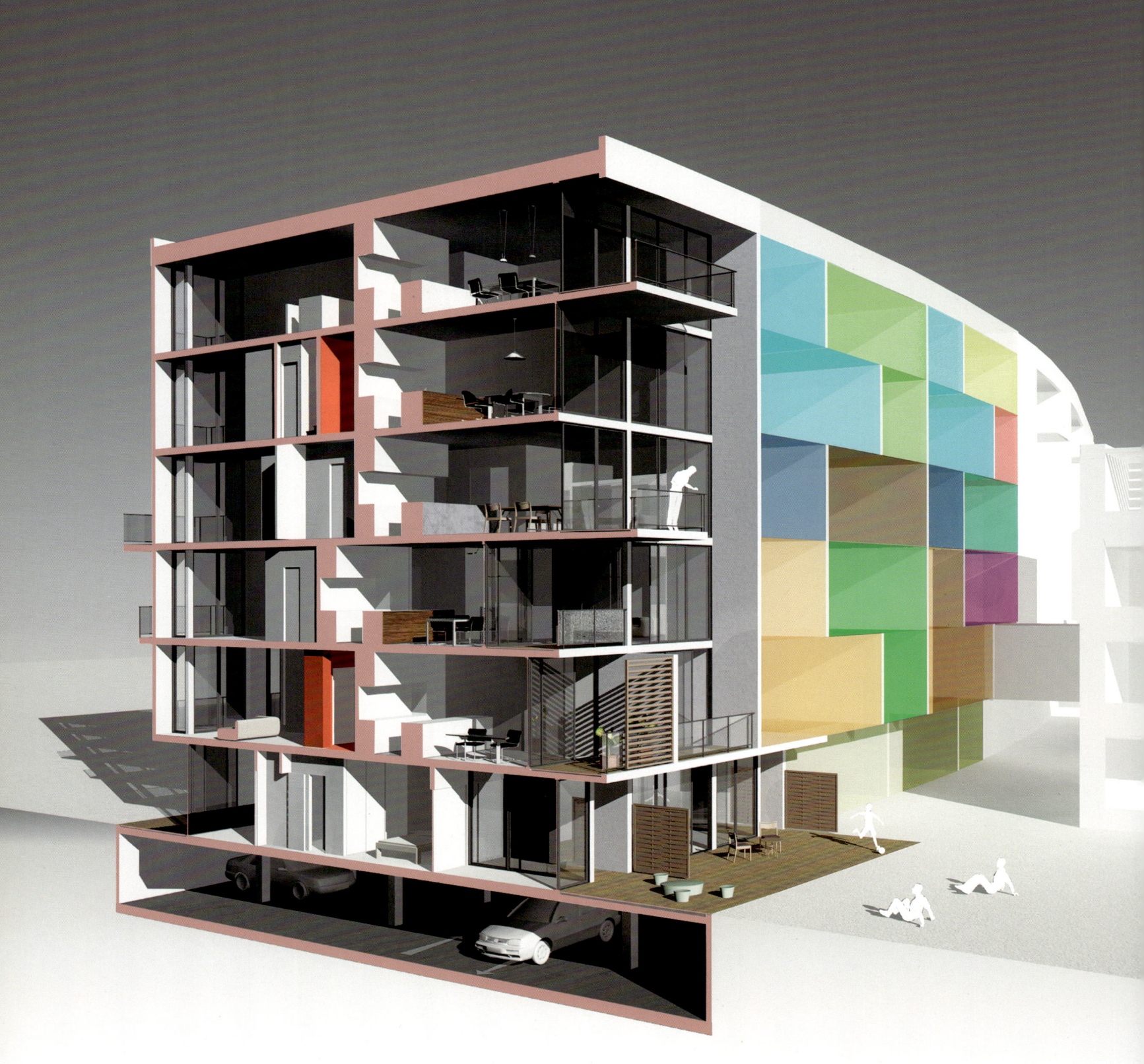

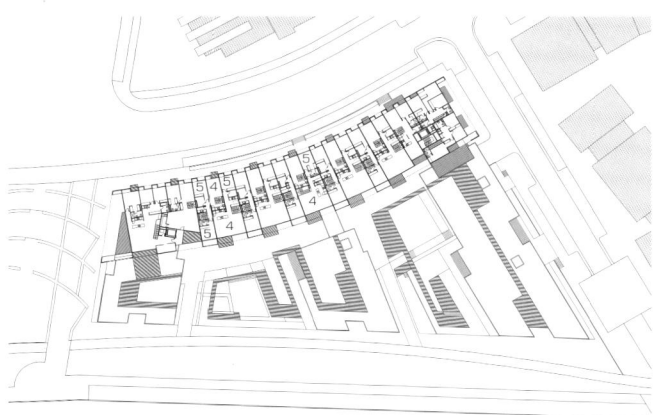

fifth floor plan

1 Lobby
2 Corridor
3 Bridge
4 Living/Dining
5 Bedroom
6 Balcony

first floor plan

third floor plan

west elevation

Wolli Creek 2003-2005

ZONE

Whilst Spectrum and Datum are what Frank Stanisic describes as "road architecture," Zone – with its southern and northern elevations facing the Illawarra and East Hills railway lines – could be described as 'rail architecture'. Located on the edge of the mangroves of Cooks River, in an area currently undergoing intensive urban renewal, Zone is one of several new housing developments replacing the existing industrial factory typology of the precinct. Although beset by the contextual difficulties of nearby factories and a floodplain, the site was ideal for high density housing, with an excellent northern aspect, views across Cooks River to the city, and close proximity to two railway stations. Conceived of as a perforated wall, Stanisic Associates proposed a permeable edge that could be repeated to the east and west of the site to form an active urban edge against the adjacent mangroves and Cooks River. Upon completion, Zone was quickly recognised as successful renewal project, which would serve as a local exemplar for sustainable high-density living.

Addressing the floodplain, with a need for open public space and an active street frontage, the project has three distinct elements: a podium, a two-storey street wall and a block-edge slab form. Raised above ground and with a northern orientation, the podium supports a public platform and courtyard, whilst on the building's southern elevation, a blood-red street wall – robust and horizontal – defines the street edge and anchors the project to its site. Rising nine storeys (with a roof terrace) behind this wall, and containing

north elevation

north elevation

62 apartments of one and two bedrooms over one, two or three storeys, the slab form is, by contrast, white and abstract. On its northern elevation, this language of insitu white concrete with deep balconies and flashes of bright sky-blue render, becomes the architect's *brise-soleil*: a patterned framework, which is more 'sky and landscape' than 'robust and industrial'. The southern elevation, with a horizontal rhythm of glazed access galleries and terraces, reconciles this white abstraction with the street and the evolving urban context. Fixed aluminium gratings are used as sun screens on the eastern and western elevations, whilst adding a finer grain to the concrete monumentality. Within each apartment, however, and in contrast to the industrial aesthetic, plantation spotted-gum timber is used for decking, and radiata pine is used for the communal courtyard's privacy screens. Water is collected from the roof and ground, then filtered and used for irrigation of the gardens and toilet flushing.

Zone is another example what Stanisic describes as 'Eco Minimalism'. Whilst the crossover sectional arrangement has its origins in the unbuilt housing schemes of the early Russian Constructivists, Stanisic observes that it was Le Corbusier who realised this organisation strategy most famously in his Unité d'Habitation. With its similar crate-like expression of concrete slab walls and balconies, and in its considerable scale, Zone recalls – perhaps more than any other of the practice's architecture – this Corbusian heritage. The Corbusian section, with its enclosed corridor, is sliced in half to create an environmentally responsive crossover plan that serves to induce airflow, generate cross-ventilation, and provide double orientation to the apartments.

site plan

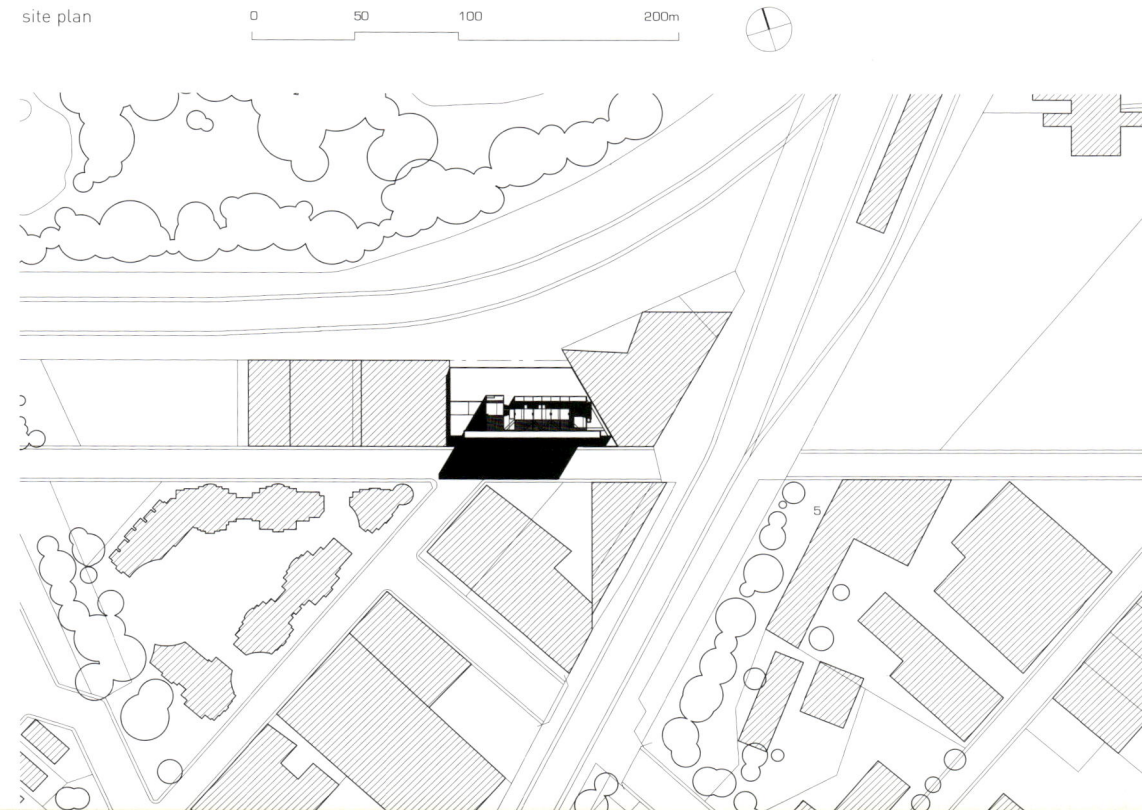

left : south elevation

following pages
left and right : north elevation
centre : circulation gallery

1 Lobby
2 Gallery
3 Balcony
4 Living/Dining
5 Bedroom

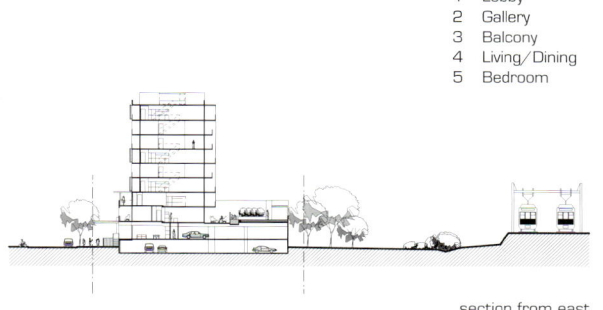

section from east

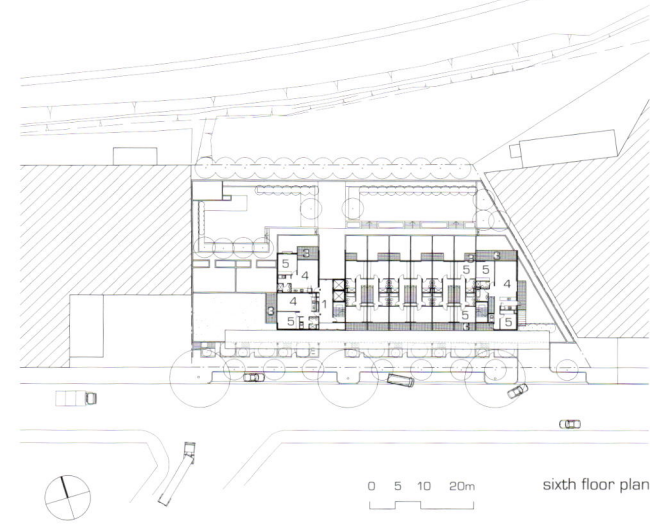

sixth floor plan

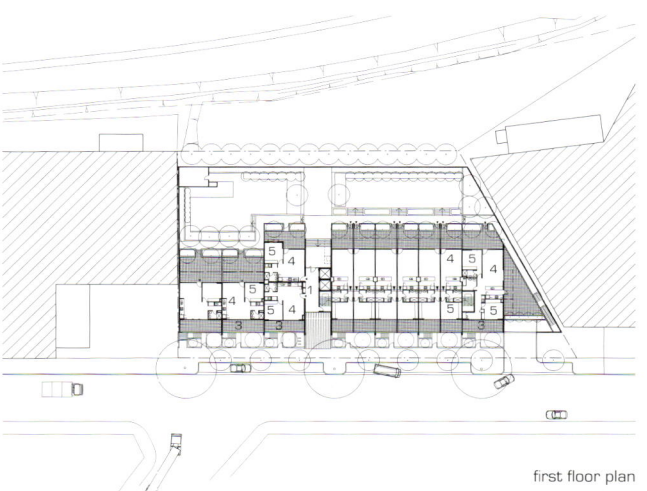

first floor plan

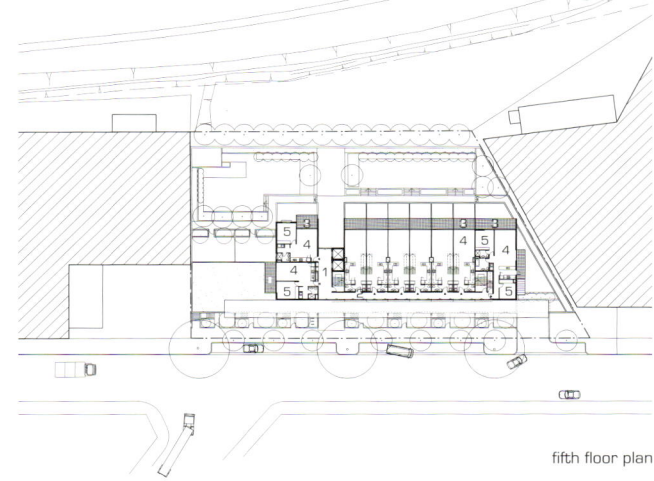

fifth floor plan

Woolloomooloo 2005-2007
EDO

Like their earlier Mondrian project, EDO represents another significant breakthrough for Stanisic Associates. With the clarity and precision of its tectonics, planning and conceptual intent, this exemplary project demonstrates the potential of compact and sustainable inner city living. In a move away from expressive concrete and a formal language that makes the programmatic and sectional complexities clearly legible on a building's exterior, EDO is far more abstract and elemental. The dominant Crown Street elevation is almost diagrammatic: a simple steel framework is 'skinned' with retractable aluminium louvre blinds. As Frank Stanisic states, each occupant received "a frame and one big space that could be individually modified and adjusted." The complexity remains within the interior, whilst the exterior – a kinetic and floating abstract box, reflective and shimmering during the day, and glowing and vibrant at night – establishes a contextual dialogue with the busy streetscape. A restaurant, located at ground level and spanning the length of building, becomes animated at night with coloured LED lighting, and a backlit bar and counter.

In this move towards an amplified abstraction and an even more formally restrained architecture, the architect's motivation is simply to create a framework for 'atmospheres', for a dwelling that allows for a myriad of individual particularities. As part of this study, EDO explores a new plan form that, inspired by Japanese moveable *shoji* screens, uses slide-away translucent walls to create another spatial dynamic and degree of flexibility: beds can be folded away, and the rooms can be opened up for alternative

west elevation

west elevation

modes of living or social requirements. The building comprises 31 single and double storey apartments of one, two and three bedrooms, with and without studies. Balconies are unusually generous at three metres, and looking out to spectacular city views and the western sun, the roof terraces are larger again at four metres, and screened by operable aluminium louvre blinds. Plantation hardwood timber is used for these outdoor spaces, which serve to extend the living area to the building's frameless glass balustrade perimeter.

Another innovation, the gallery, is to be found on EDO's eastern side, at the threshold between the interior and the lush courtyard. Replacing the practice's typical access gallery system, this two storey-high mezzanine gallery, with fixed open louvres, creates a generous well-ventilated space that serves as a community meeting point and as access for the lower two levels of apartments. Cool air is drawn from the garden, through the gallery, through small louvres located above the apartments' entry doors, and then through the apartment to the building's western side. The upper two levels are accessed via a central corridor lined with reflective surfaces, such as marble walls and metallic slotted acoustic ceiling panels. The two- and three-storey apartments wrap over the internal corridor, providing well-ventilated double orientated apartments and maximising the captivating views of the city skyline. When read from an eastern vantage point, the building takes on an almost Eames-like sensibility: a wall of milky-white glazing, steel-framed with fine aluminium mullion detailing, sits atop the gallery's louvred wall.

In keeping with the architecture's spatial and conceptual elegance, the entry lobby is simple and understated, finished with concrete and MDF acoustic panels. Only the huge perforated metal rings of Peter McGregor's public art installation, set against a bright red backdrop, give a more formal indication of entrance. EDO is an acronym for Environment, Diversity, and Operability, and the application of these principles – designing compact collective housing in an environmentally responsive manner, creating a diversity of apartment types suitable for the city's demographic mix, and providing occupant flexibility through the operability of screens, walls and openings – serves as a prototype for accommodating Sydney's rapidly increasing population.

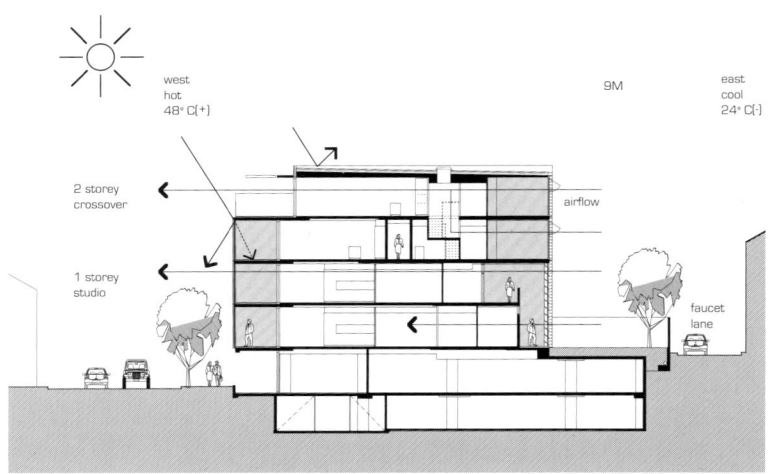

summer solstice

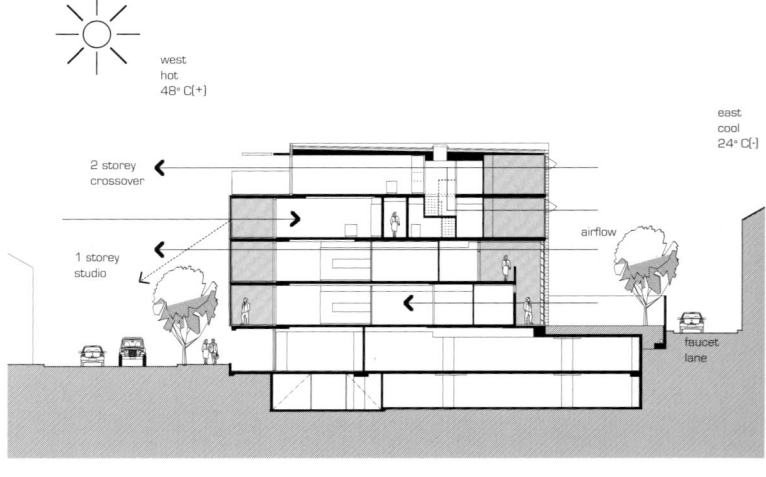

winter solstice

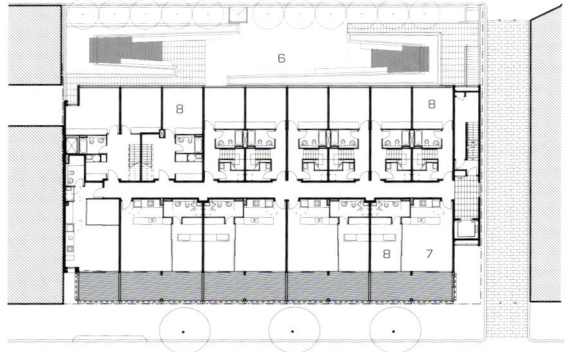

fourth floor plan

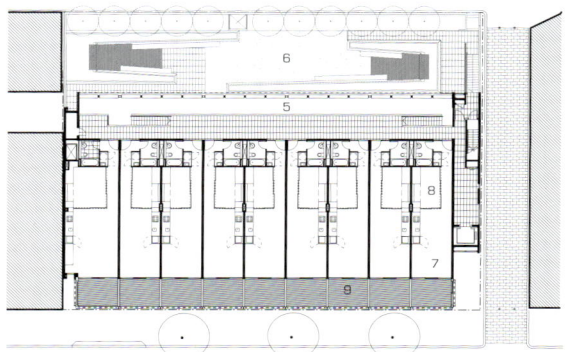

fifth floor plan

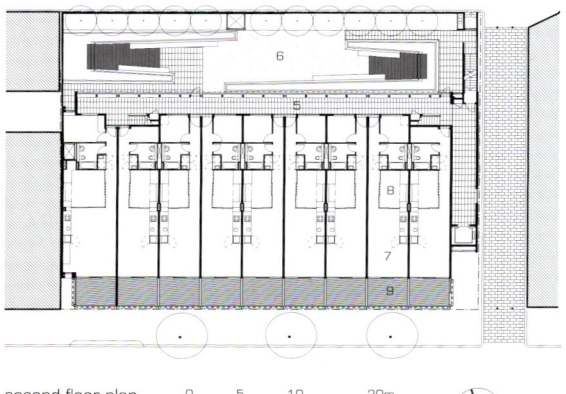

second floor plan   0 5 10 20m

third floor plan

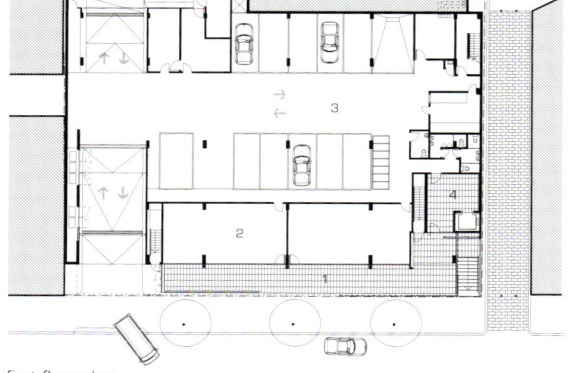

first floor plan

1 Retail Terrace
2 Retail
3 Parking
4 Lobby
5 Gallery
6 Courtyard
7 Living/Dining
8 Bedroom
9 Loggia

west elevation

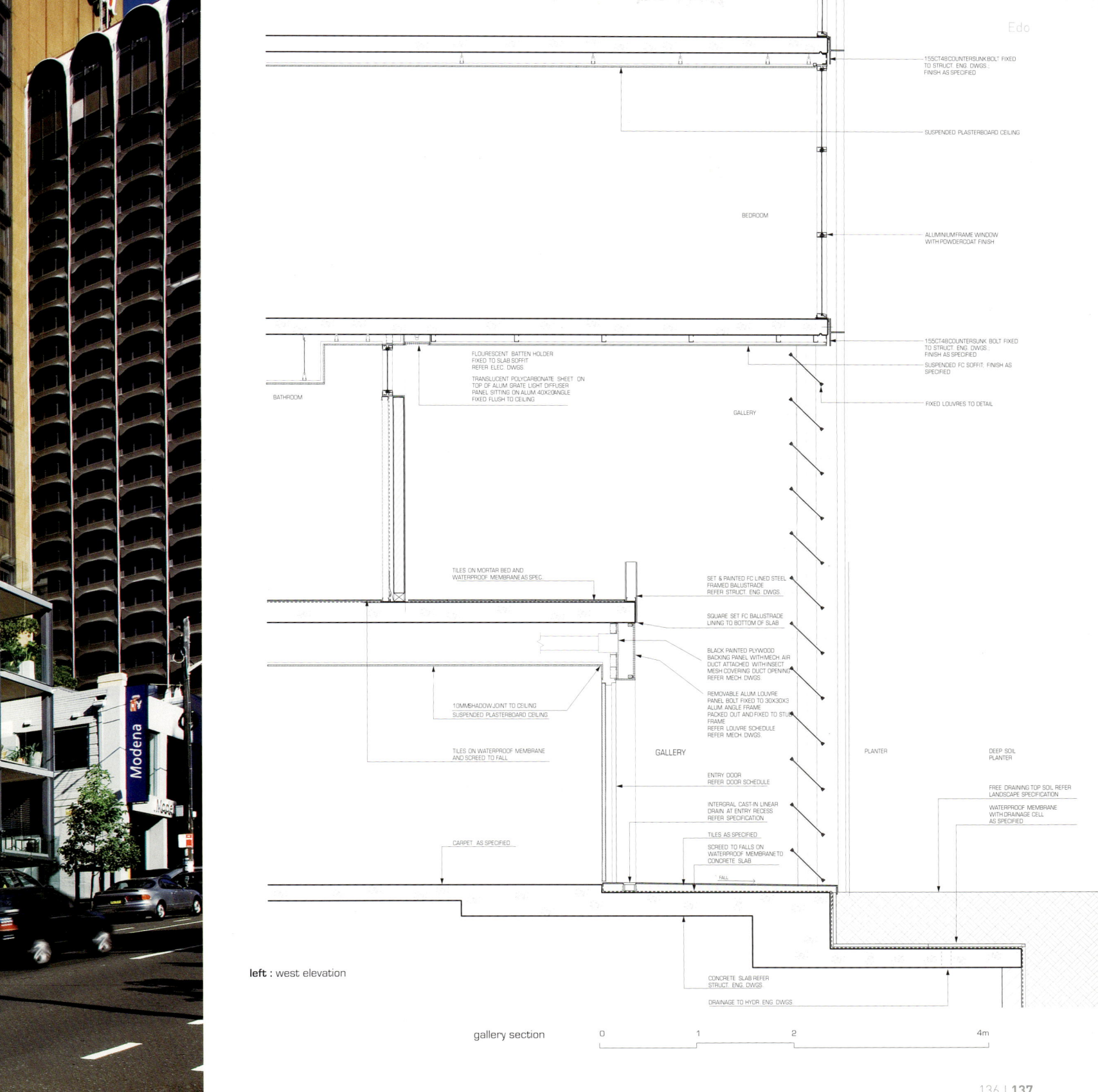

left : west elevation

gallery section

above : east elevation **centre** : central corridor
right : eastern mezzanine gallery

following pages
right : eastern mezzanine gallery **all other**
images : typical apartment interiors

Tom Heneghan

edo

Tom Heneghan is Professor
of Architectural Design,
Department of Architecture,
Tokyo University and former
Chair of Architecture, University
of Sydney

Article published in Architecture
Australia, May/June 2007,
Vol. 96, No. 3

An important shift is taking place in contemporary architectural practice, one which the NSW awards program at both state and national levels is beginning to recognise. Over the last few years a number of medium density projects have won major awards for residential architecture in categories that had previously acknowledged only the design of individual houses. In 2003, the NSW jury, recognising the immense and growing importance of collective housing and its influence on the quality of the urban environment, awarded 'twin' Wilkinson Awards - one to the rural, isolated, Toumbaal Plains House by Fergus Scott, and one to Mondrian by Frank Stanisic, a city centre housing development of mid-price-level apartments of an elegance and invention that very profoundly raised the bar.

In Sydney – a city of burgeoning population and high land values – and in the environmental situation in which we now find ourselves, the apartment building, rather than the single house on the quarter-acre block, must increasingly become the appropriate residential-type, even outside those areas that pass for the city's urban centres. In order to maintain relevance, architects must increasingly address the issue of collective living: a concern that has been neglected in recent decades, but which transfixed the architects of early and mid-period Modernism, although their successes in that area, it must be said, were few. Housing of international quality has arisen in recent years, designed by some of the city's finest architects and visitors: for example Horizon, Moore Park Gardens, Altair, Walsh Bay: Victoria Park, META, Aurora Place, and Stanisic's many lauded and awarded projects throughout the city. Of these, Stanisic's Mondrian was a landmark, showing how, by reason of the architect's ambition and ingenuity, quality can be achieved within the restrictions of a mid-range commercial budget. It offered cross-ventilated units with balconies of exceptional size, shaded by sliding louvres: in tune with the particular conditions and styles of life in sunny Sydney. It helped establish the 'look' of contemporary Sydney apartment living, and its many derivatives, by other hands, no matter how weak, attest to its positive influence. But perhaps its most significant contribution to the debate was its site-specificity. It incorporated an existing pedestrian public route into its variety of linked, shared garden spaces, binding it to its context, and making it part of the fabric of its city, not merely a collection of objects on a plot. As Sydney expands and densifies, such an urbanistic approach to individual architectural projects is increasingly important. The parallel issue of the manner in which housing may define the contemporary urban streetscape is addressed by Stanisic in his recent project, EDO, where he investigates a prototypical response to constricted city centre sites. Here, his intention is less the creation of a site-specific work than the creation of an exemplar. We now so esteem the indi-

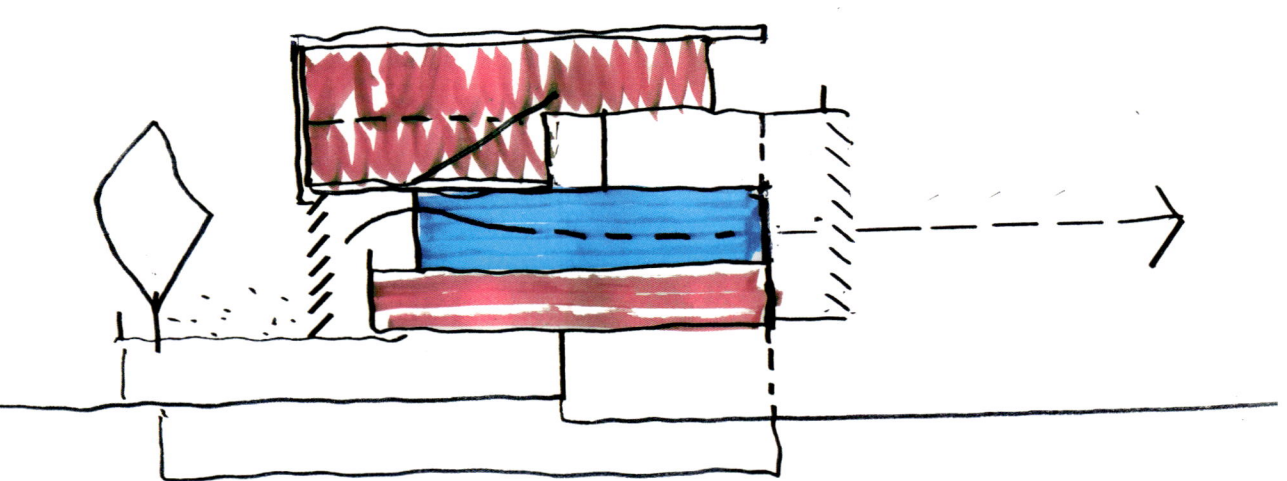

vidualist icons of the international 'starchitects' that it is easy to forget that many of the world's most significant architects – from John Nash to Le Corbusier to Team X to Christopher Alexander – focused on the creation of exemplars that informed the collective, and that it is through the application of a refined consensual orthodoxy, a typology, that cities obtain their coherence and quality. Stanisic's contribution at EDO is an essential and timely experiment in contemporary living and urban decorum. One wonders at the impact on the city would be were EDO to become – as it should – the reference point for all new medium-density housing developments across Sydney.

On a long and narrow north-south plot, addressing a busy street scene of no distinction – a typical Sydney city-centre context – Stanisic composes 31 apartments of five different types and sizes over four floors, behind a unifying grid-façade, which floats above a recessed base. The grid gives order to the façade, but also gives an intentional ambiguity: the considerable cantilever implies the lightness of steel construction, and the crisp metallic framing around the balconies contributes to this misreading of the in-situ concrete. This steelwork, in fact, provides the housing and tracking for individually controllable louvre screens, giving each balcony innumerable possible degrees of differing enclosure or exposure: from being a clearly separate external space to being the enclosed, most naturally-ventilated section of the living room, with which, cleverly detailed, it shares its floor-level. The differently tuned screens of each balcony, together with the slightly altered structural grid and roll-out canopies of the top floor terraces, give this apparently very simply ordered building a very rich, animated 'flicker' as its character oscillates between the systematic and the jaunty. The building has a linear central section which elegantly provides for the essentials of habitation. This has an attached cushioning layer of external space on each side: individual balconies to the west, and to the east (the rear) a tall communal gallery from which the lower two floors of apartments are accessed. This gallery, which faces into a small, but very well landscaped, private garden, is only semi-enclosed by widely-spaced horizontal glass louvres, giving it the character of a wintergarden. This is effectively an external space, of a scale and width to invite casual use and children's play, which permits the apartments that open from it to take natural ventilation from both sides. On the top two floors, the apartments are accessed by a more conventional corridor at third-floor level, opening to double-fronted apartments to the west, and to double-storey apartments, entered to the east, which wrap over the corridor to give the principal rooms and their canopied terraces panoramic western views over the Domain and the CBD. Within the unifying system of the building envelope, there is a flexibility that enables the bringing together of very different, prototypical, apartment layouts, in which the central criterion is the provision of natural ventilation.

Edo - Tom Heneghan

The apartments are meticulously planned with an easy sophistication: interior space in this inner-city site is at a premium, and Stanisic, as he has done with some previous works, enables the individual 'tuning' of the smallest interiors by the use of sliding translucent screen walls that subdivide the space into bed and living spaces, or allow it to be opened up and perceived as one. A consistent language of additive detailing unites all parts of the building at all scales: from the approach where one 'slides' into the entrance behind a glass screen that is applied to the façade, to the manner in which the drawers and doors are designed to 'float' within the carcasses of the kitchen furniture. And in the general neutrality of the whole – simple, often silent – materials are invited to 'speak' eloquently: the apparently dense, though not actual, timber that lines the elevator lobbies, the marble sheets that line one side of the upper interior corridor, and the simple repetitive perforation patterns of the sound-absorbing panels that are attached to slab soffits. Despite the fineness of its aesthetic, the design of EDO is driven by use, not by appearance. In electing for – or being obliged to accept – apartment dwelling, the sense of identity and territory that Australians have typically found so appealing in the quarter-acre block, is forfeited. Mondrian, for all its qualities, presented no particular solutions to this dilemma. But it is in this that EDO is most innovative. Although the apartments are generally narrower – and more 'urban' – than those of Mondrian, the very significant adjustments each resident can make to their interior layout and balcony, and to the way that both are perceived, provide a significant sense of individual identity within the collective, and a sense of self-determination and control of one's own residential environment.

Stanisic is arguably Sydney's most notable current exponent of collective housing design, and EDO is an eloquent exposition of his understanding of this building type and its budgeting, and of his ability to exploit the potential – not the loopholes – of its particular legislation. The filigreed motorised balcony screening, which can so very dramatically transform the sense of space of each apartment, merely modifies sunlight and privacy, and to a degree, wind, but the balcony is at all times external space – never in conflict with the planning allowance – and offers residents a usable living space far larger than the interior area they have paid for. It's the same with the 'wintergarden' access gallery, which, despite the qualities it contributes to the residential experience, is in fact only modified external environment. EDO demonstrates a rare cleverness, ingenuity and ambition in the provision of collective housing, and a vision for its place in the contemporary urban streetscape.

Kings Cross 2005-2009
ERA

With its 5 star ABGR energy rating, Era is one of only a handful of mixed-use office buildings in Sydney that have achieved this level of environmental sustainability without resorting to the purchase of green credits. Occupying an infill site in the gritty urban context of Kings Cross, this seven-storey building holds 44 office strata modules, a ground floor level with fifteen shops and a supermarket, a communal courtyard, basement parking and an energy efficient substation. Envisaged as a low-energy passive environment that accommodates a 'loose fit' sustainable working and shopping enclave, all offices are naturally lit and ventilated. Comprised of two slim-line buildings running east-west with a through-site public pedestrian way between Springfield Avenue and Llankelly Place, Era is one of Stanisic Associates' most sophisticated mixed-use office buildings.

In a transformation of the Sydney arcade type, a covered public throughway that may once have held a number of floors lined with shops now becomes a passively designed breezeway with gallery walkways for pedestrian access to the offices. The breezeway – vertically contained by fine metal gridded screens below an angled, glazed louvred roof – operates as a thermal stack: this space is an essential element of the building's passive design, collecting cool breezes, which are drawn through to the offices by dampers located at their entry. The roof system, angled so that it lets out the hot air whilst protecting from heavy rains, bathes the arcade with sunlight. Each office has a three-metre balcony, whilst a series of operable glass louvre screens defines the building's north

central breezeway

west elevation

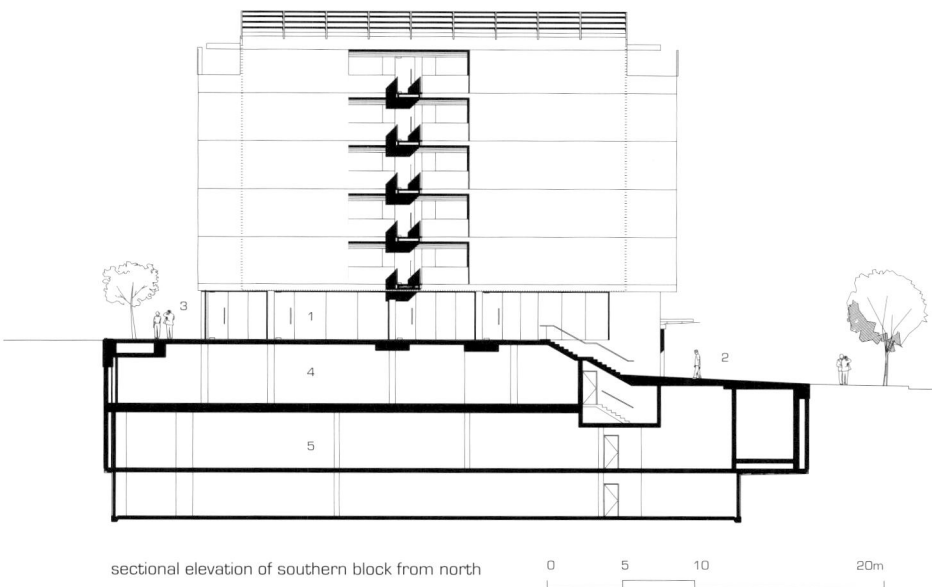

sectional elevation of southern block from north

0 5 10 20m

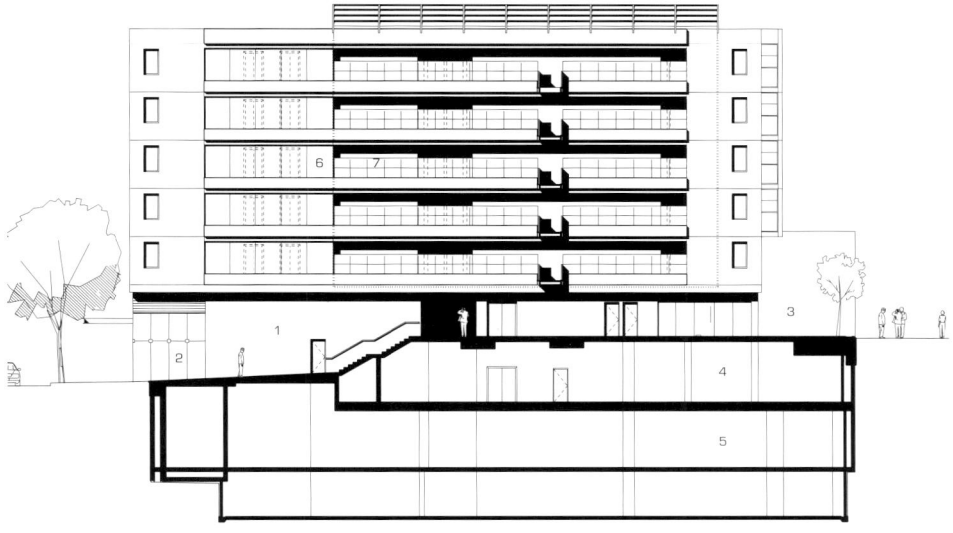

sectional elevation of northern block from south

elevation and encourages modification of the office spaces in reaction to the weather and the time of day. Providing a SOHO-like environment, all offices have a service pod that contains a small bathroom, a kitchenette, a data hub and a recycling store, and the flexible wall construction between suites means that an entire floor could be opened up for one occupant or company.

Through a very careful configuration of enclosed and open spaces, the breezeway can be technically classified as an exterior space, which permits flexible design of the office doors and pods. Without the requirement for solid fire-safe doors or compartmentalised pods, the threshold between office and breezeway can be more variable, containing the dampers and openings essential for the cross-ventilation and 'breathability' of the offices. A communal and protected courtyard space lies on the northern ground level, whilst the building's interiors – in contrast to the robust planar appearance of the exterior – become cool, tempered spaces with varying degrees of light and a rich combination of colour and material. An industrial palette of aluminium screens, concrete and glass is embellished with timber benches, red-wine toned tiles and the warm glow of LED lighting, whilst the exterior forms a solid armature that addresses the realities of the local context: it is, as Frank Stanisic says, "a protecting shell."

1 Breezeway/Pedestrian Way
2 Forecourt
3 Retail Terrace
4 Supermarket
5 Parking
6 Lobby
7 Access Gallery

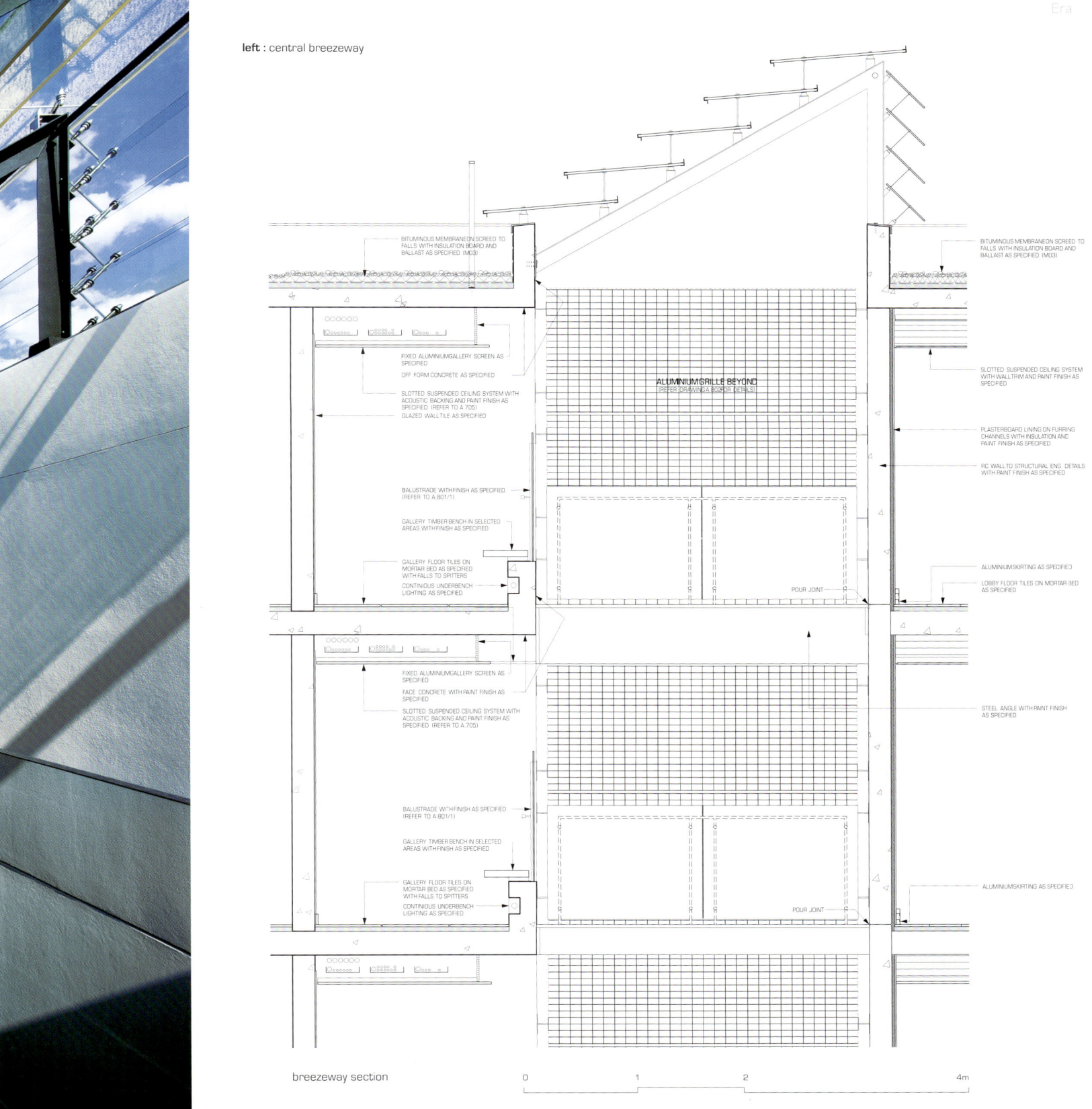

left : central breezeway

breezeway section

view from northwest

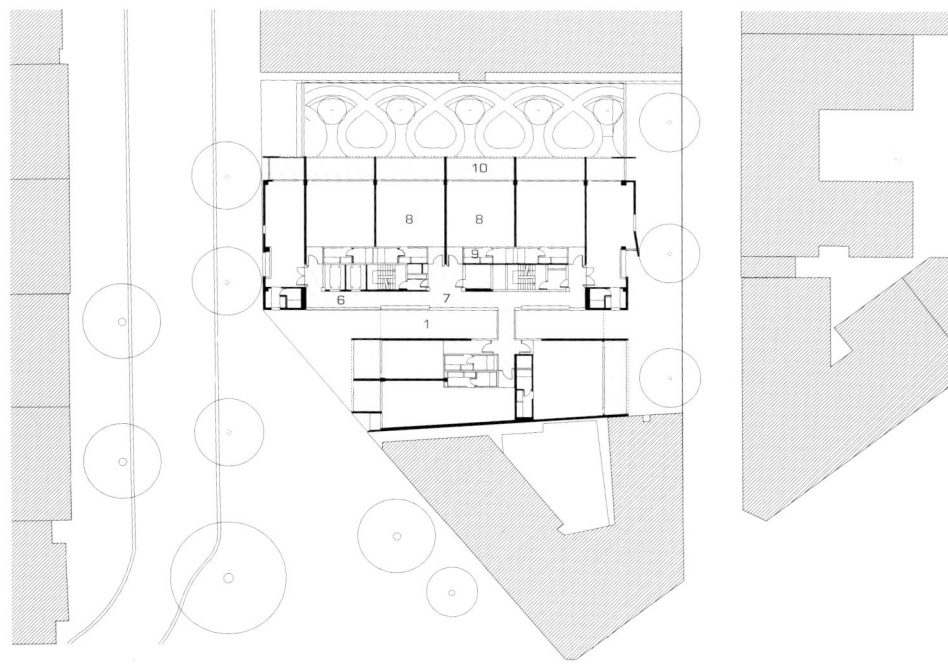

typical upper floor plan

1 Breezeway
2 Forecourt
3 Retail Terrace
4 Minor Arcade
5 Retail
6 Lobby
7 Access Gallery
8 Office
9 Service Pod
10 Loggia

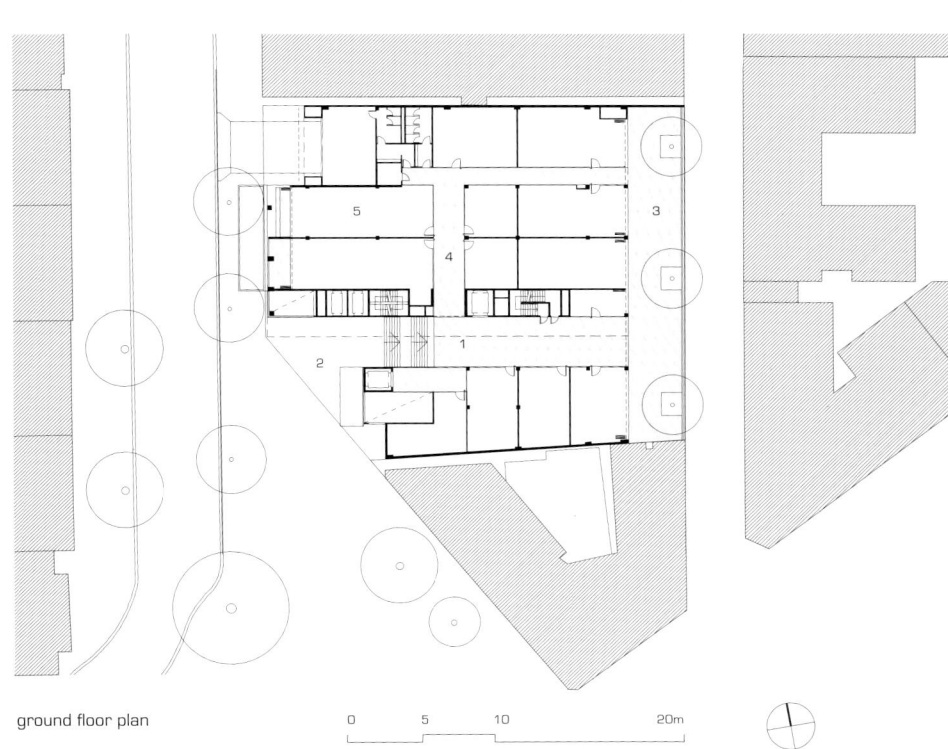

ground floor plan

0 5 10 20m

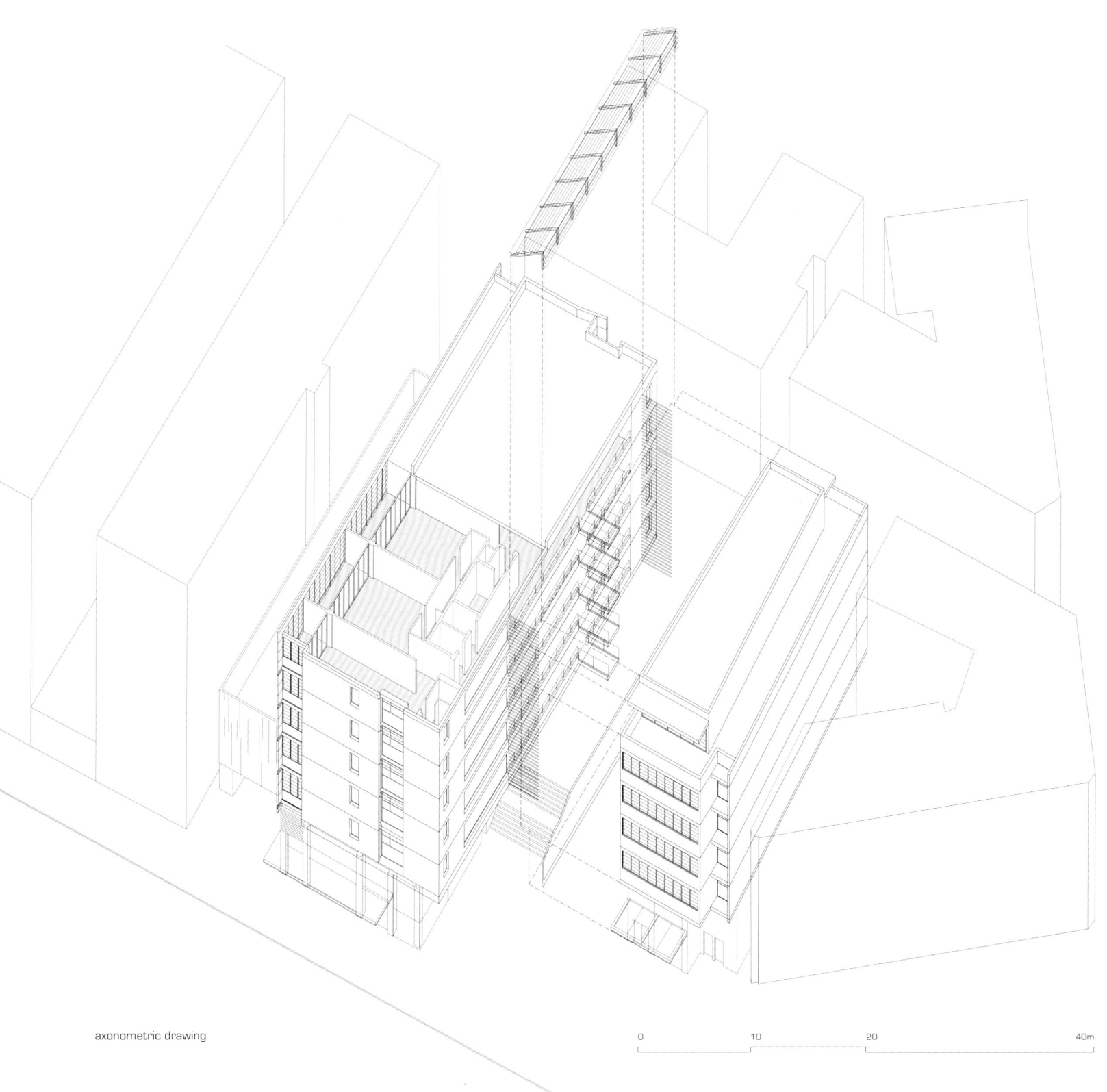
axonometric drawing

view from northeast

above : north elevation centre and right : central breezeway

following pages
above right : roof over breezeway **below centre right** : entry foyer **below right** : breezeway tiles
all other images : typical office interiors

left : north elevation from courtyard
right : northern courtyard

Rosebery 2005 (unbuilt)
DUNNING

Although the studio of Stanisic Associates has a strong reputation for collective housing, the practice is becoming increasingly involved with the investigation of hybrid typologies and with questions of appropriate formal expression. It is becoming increasingly evident that the program itself is not the critical issue for the design of sustainable, environmentally responsive architecture. Alternatively, in more recent explorations, the formal idea is not tied to a particular program, but is conceived of as a framework for accommodation and for a variety of programs and events. The building is as equally engaged in establishing contextual urban relationships and responsibilities as it is with providing an environmentally responsive and flexible interior. Projects such as Quay and Waterside illustrate this shift, and the conceptual armature for Dunning is that of an 'environmental filter', prescribing an innovative sustainable building that facilitates social exchange, has a low energy consumption, and allows people to work in 'unplugged' offices. The proposed office environment is therefore both interactive and informal: offering an alternative to the traditional office spaces of mute 'over-engineered' enclosures dislocated from their environment.

Located at the southern end of the Green Square urban renewal area, Dunning – with a slender L-shaped block running parallel to Epsom Road – intentionally becomes an integrated response to the microenvironment of the South Sydney/Botany Bay area: interior and exterior are in a relationship of reciprocity, with 'breathing spaces' responding to daily climatic conditions. The raised ground floor level, which is positioned above the flood

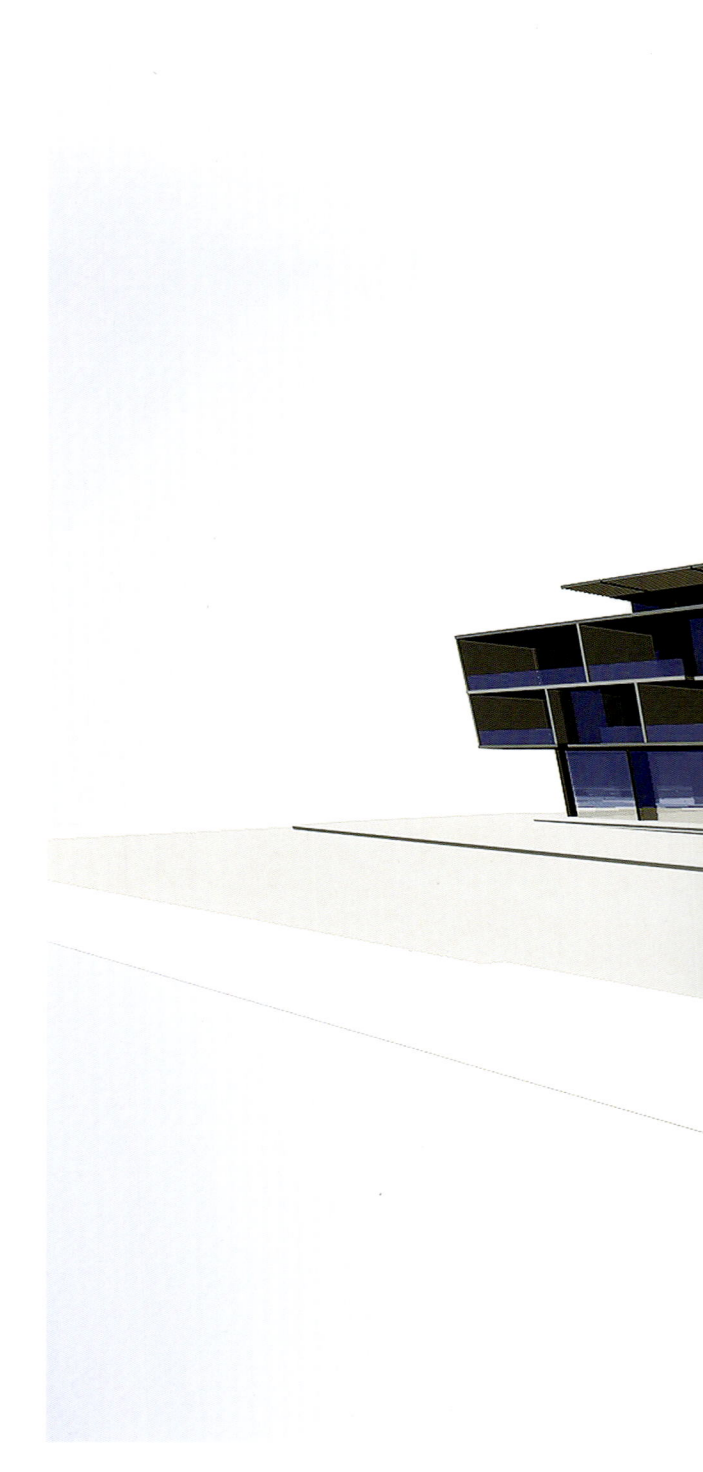

level of the site, forms an urban terrace containing an entry lobby, retail spaces and a café, with a communal courtyard tucked in to the building's southern side, below three office levels. Serving as a place of solitude or conversation for workers and as an extension of the public ground floor activities, the courtyard – planted with trees – forms part of an integrated and sustainable system, whereby cool air is drawn into the open access 'breathing' galleries – similar to the principle of the EDO gallery – that run behind the north-facing offices. All offices have access to three metre balconies and, at the top level, larger offices have access to roof terraces. Conceived of as a long life, loose fit, low energy (LL:LF:LE) environment, the building comprises a 'matrix' of column-free spaces with a generous ceiling height of 3.6 metres. The offices can be joined or separated as required, and each office module has a service pod containing toilets, a shower, a basin, and kitchenettes.

As viewed from Epsom Road, the north-facing elevation reads as a floating sliver grey box: muscular, abstract and devoid of pretention, with coherence and detail provided by the familiar crate-like *brise soleil* structure found in the residential projects of the practice. This office box is further articulated with zinc cladding, and contrasts with the concrete frame of the *brise soleil* and with a series of fixed aluminium louvres. Set back in accordance with local planning regulations, the top level of offices reads as a continuous glazed strip with a floating roof, whilst the southern elevation, from which the open access galleries are visible, appears as a more planar surface, articulated with the ribbon-like strips of the galleries and the glazing of the top-storey offices. The overall building establishes a strong southern edge to Epsom Road, whilst activating the ground level: extending the conditions established by the neighbouring Coda, also by Stanisic Associates.

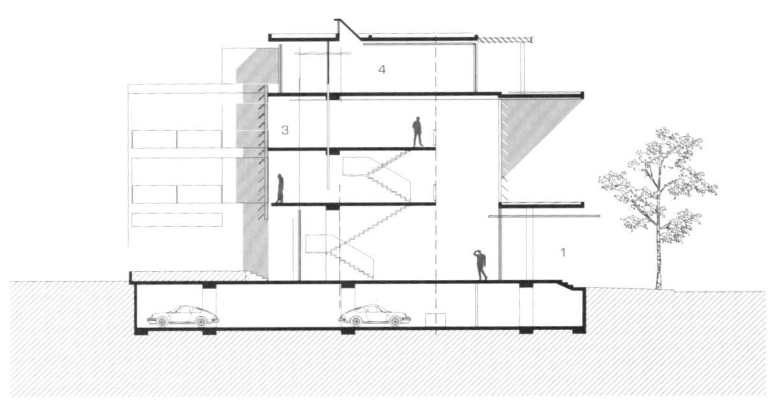

section from east

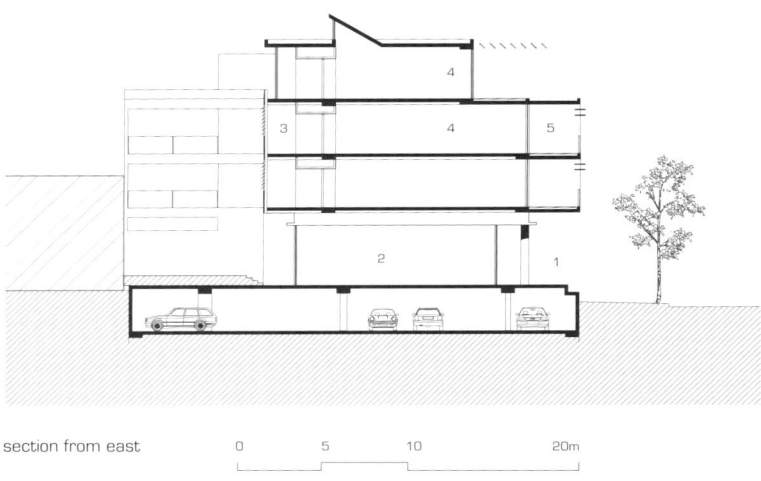

section from east

1 Retail Terrace
2 Retail
3 Gallery
4 Offices
5 Loggia

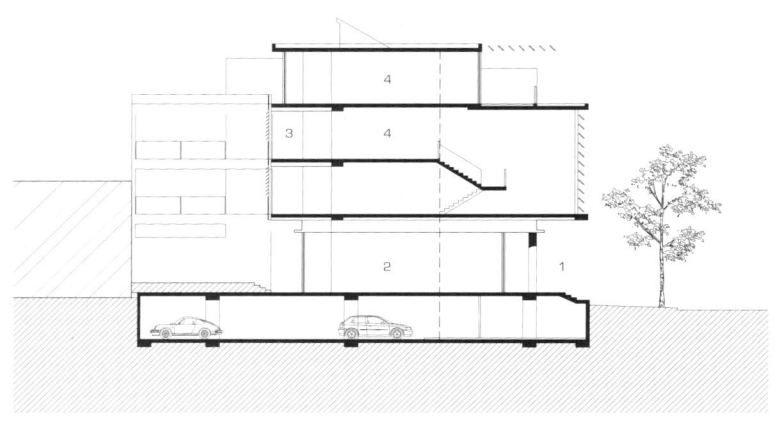

section from east

right and right above: north elevation

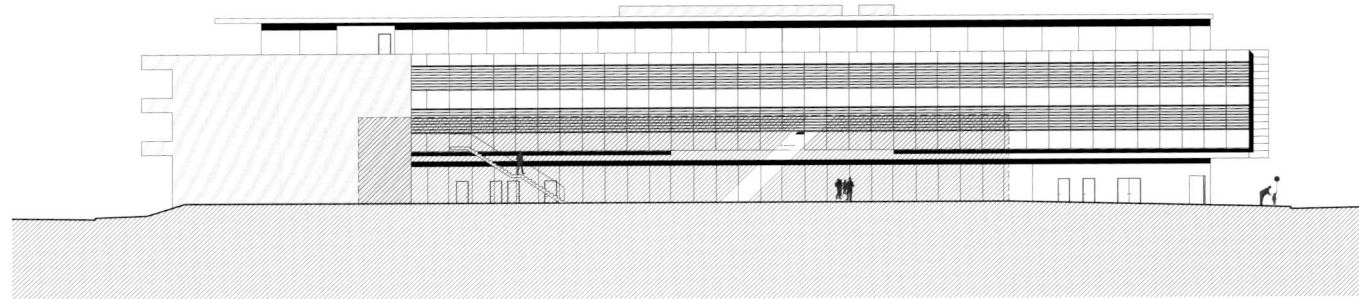

south elevation

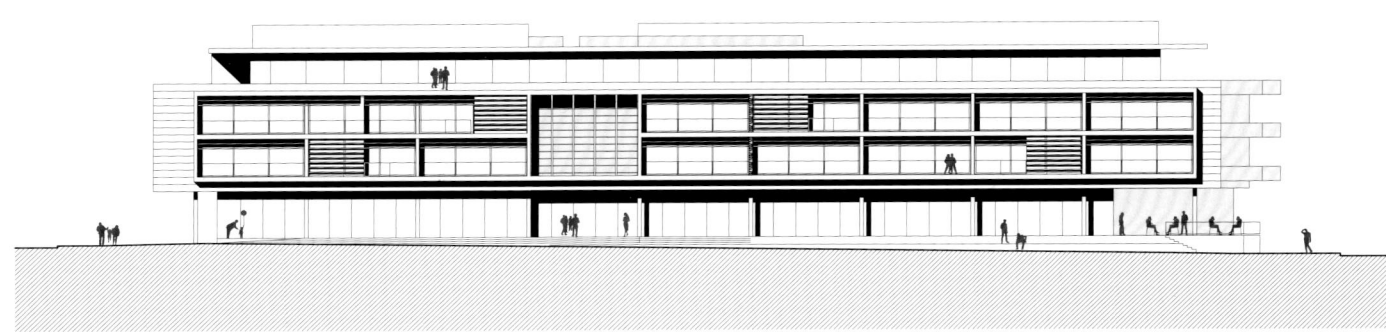

north elevation

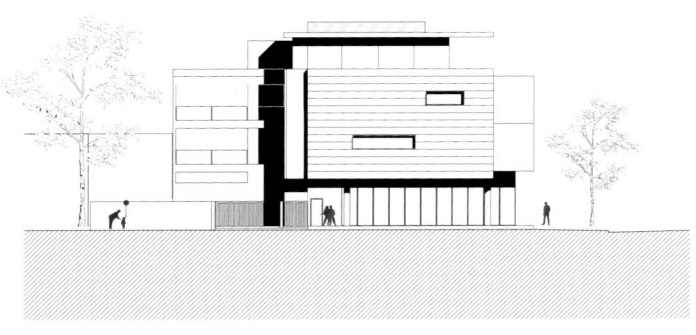

east elevation

0 5 10 20m

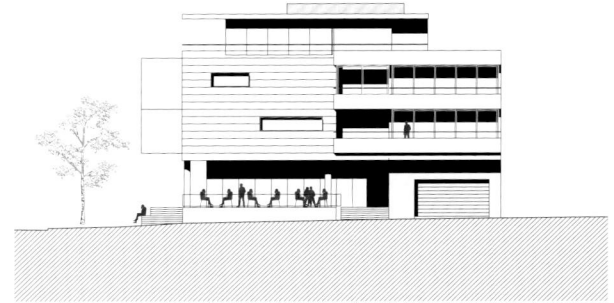

west elevation

1 Retail Terrace
2 Retail
3 Lobby
4 Courtyard
5 Gallery
6 Offices
7 Loggia

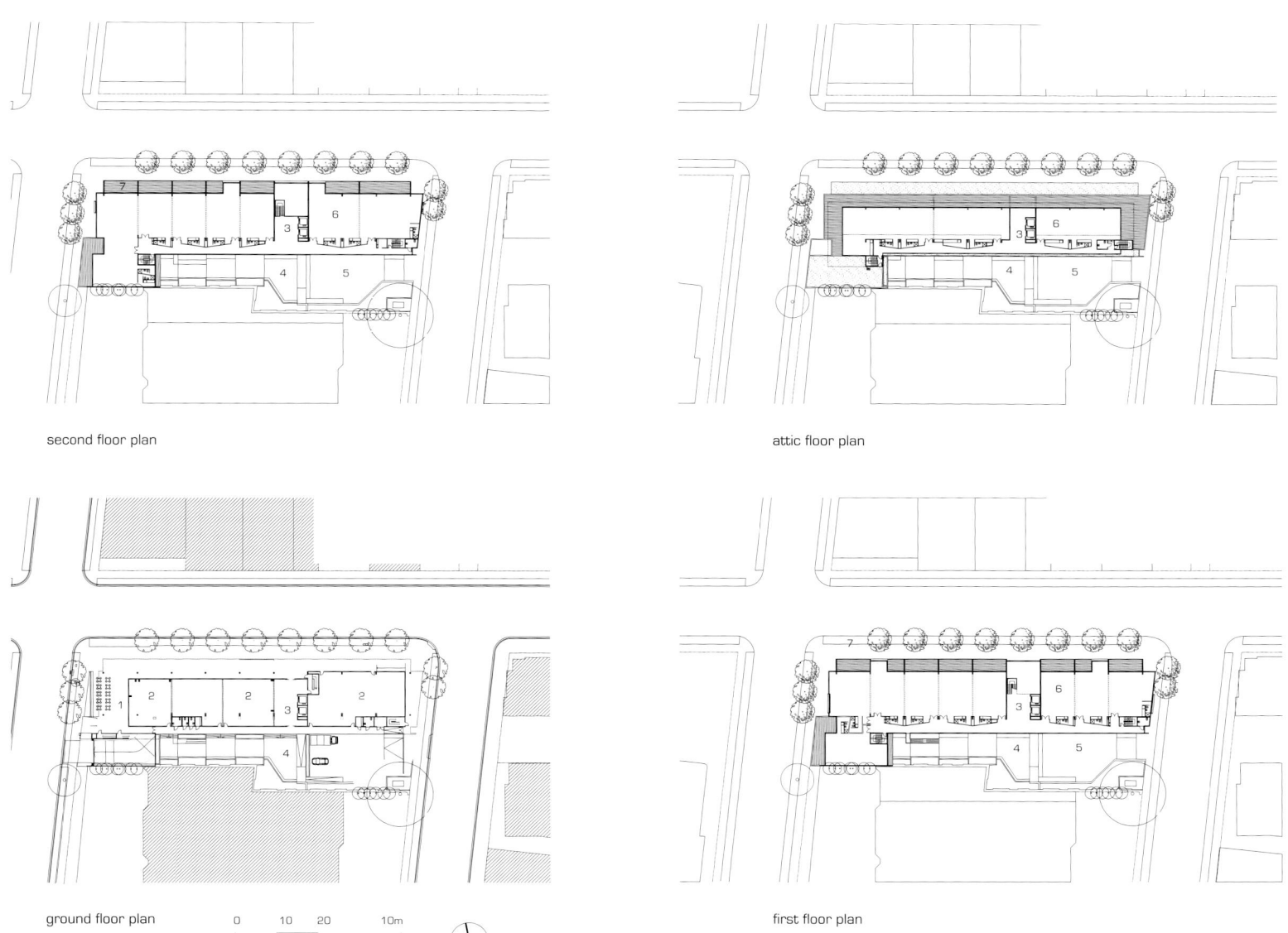

second floor plan

attic floor plan

ground floor plan

first floor plan

Little Bay 2006 (unbuilt)
PRINCE HENRY

A multi-unit project, comprised of two building blocks, is positioned on the northwest corner of the Prince Henry redevelopment of a former hospital site in the southeastern suburbs of Sydney. Perched on a ridge with views of Little Bay and Botany Bay to the west, the development runs along Anzac Parade and across Gubbeteh Road and, whilst occupying two sides of Gubbeteh Road, the project – with 54 apartments over five storeys and a pattern of communal courtyards – was conceived of 'in the round', and as one development. The dominant building blocks running along Anzac Parade are further examples of 'road architecture', recalling such earlier Stanisic Associates projects as Datum and Spectrum. The expression of 'stretched' planar surfaces, interrupted by entrance lobbies and strip windows, establishes an urban edge to Anzac Parade, as well as providing the rear elevations with a northeasterly aspect, sea breezes, and views to the coastline of Little Bay from living spaces with generous balconies.

Whilst at first glance, these apartments possess a simple, restrained aesthetic, their architectural conception is explicitly concerned with passive environmental performance and with creating a durable and low maintenance 'coastal' expression that complements the surrounding landscape. Constructed from precast concrete panels, contrasting with lightweight prefinished aluminium cladding, this language of seaside ambience is further articulated by sliding aluminium plantation shutters fixed to expansive balconies, and by the ribbon windows used on the Anzac Parade elevation. A palette of soft whites and greys, with sandstone and native flora tones, has been used for accents and highlights.

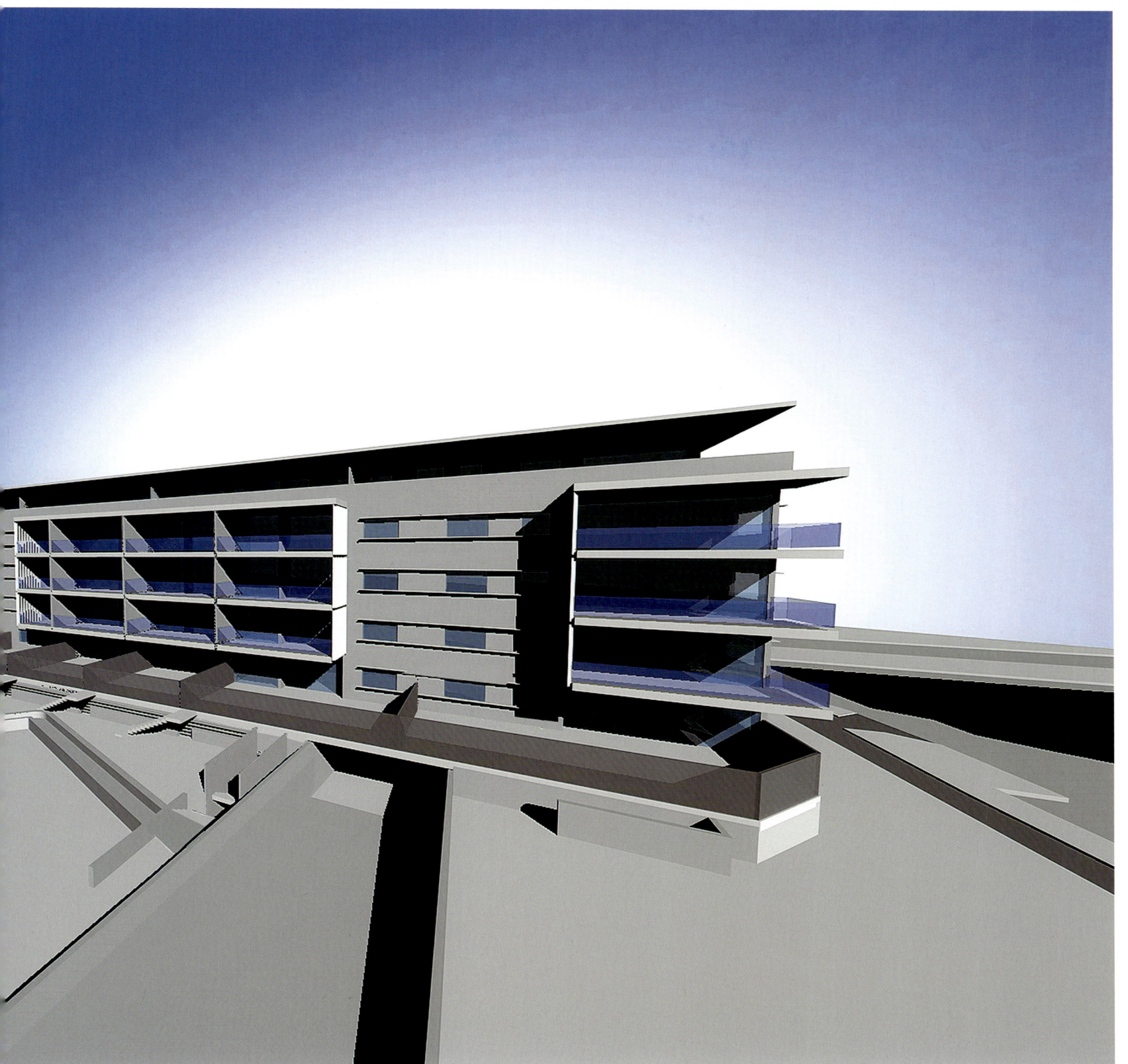

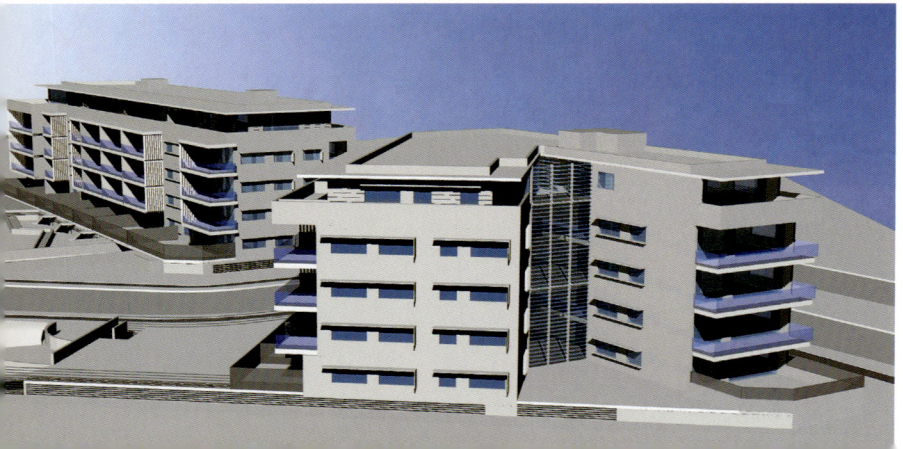

Aiming to address the area's mixed demographic – with a high percentage of 'empty nesters' – provision is made for mainly two, or three, bedroom apartments on a single level. Top level 'loft apartments' are larger with protected roof terraces, and communal courtyards are planted with local native plants, with a permeable ground cover, and with seating and walking paths. The project incorporates grey water treatment to reduce the use of potable water, and recycled water will be used to irrigate gardens, flush toilets and wash cars. Gas powered energy generation for hot water is boosted by solar collectors, and electrical energy for communal lighting is generated by photovoltaic panels: all located on the concrete roofs of the lofts.

The northern block, with a more irregular shaped boundary and a shorter frontage to Anzac Parade, has two double-storey wintergardens between the east and west wings: placed at ground level, these external gardens – protected by fixed glass louvres – are connected to the adjoining apartments with operable louvres to form part of the natural airflow system. This modest project possesses humble, but important, ambitions to create a sustainable, climatically responsive architecture, based on passive design principles, whilst addressing the immediate context and landscape conditions.

anzac parade elevation

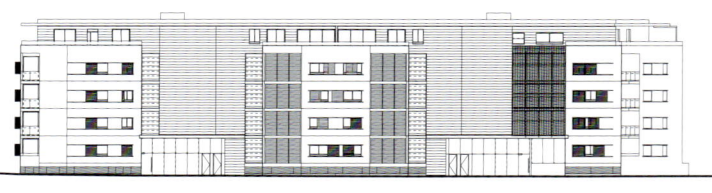

courtyard elevation

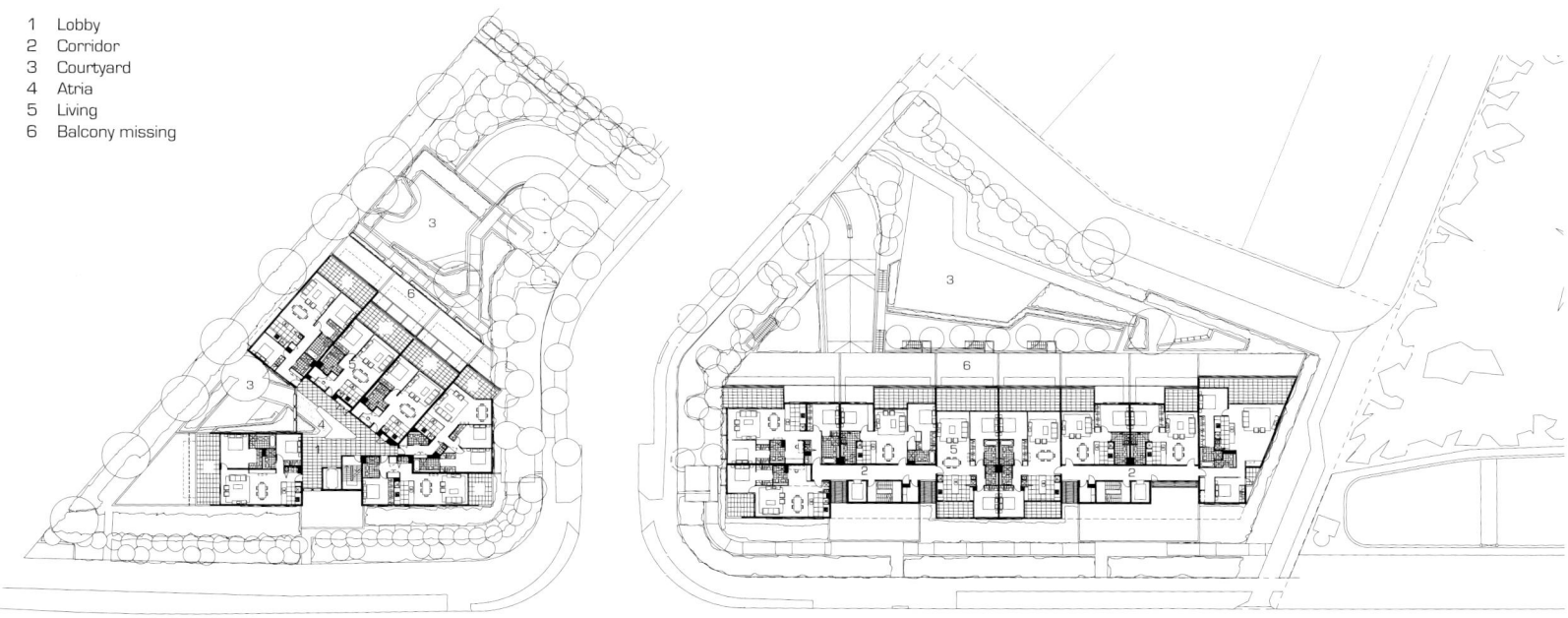

1 Lobby
2 Corridor
3 Courtyard
4 Atria
5 Living
6 Balcony missing

first floor plan

ground floor plan 0 5 10 20m

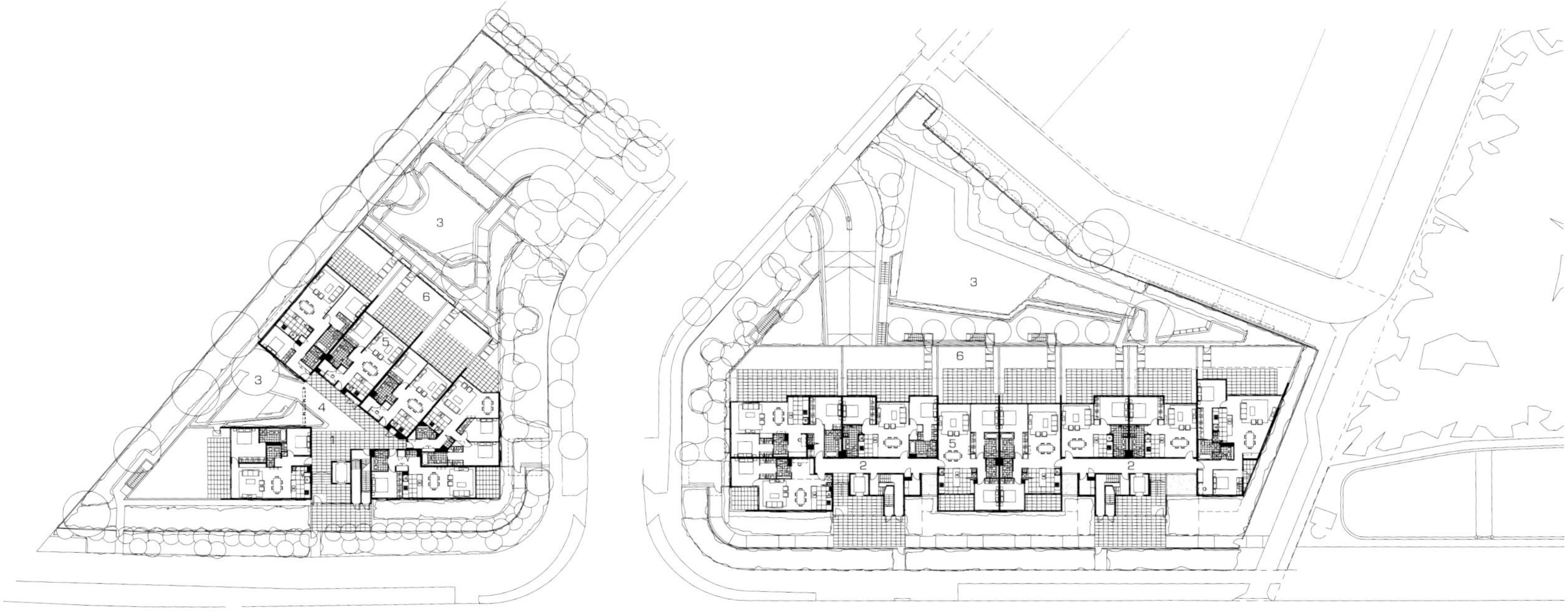

Haymarket 2008 (unbuilt)
QUAY

This proposal for the redevelopment of an inner city site on the corner of Quay and Thomas Streets entailed the demolition of an existing ten-storey commercial car park, which was to be replaced with a fourteen-storey mixed-use office building and a ten-level underground car park. Continuing Stanisic Associates' explorations of an abstract but restorative urban form, Quay demonstrates a robust architecture that evolved from the particular site conditions. Having a singular formal presence, it possesses an abstraction that speaks of the material and the structural technologies, as well as the potential of an adaptable 'diagrammatic' tectonic: one that is not referential, and establishes its own systems and rule base.

Whilst the site, located in the thriving inner city area of Haymarket, possesses a programmatic diversity and is well serviced by public transport, it is surrounded – as with many inner city sites – by a messy agglomeration of building styles, sizes, materials and character. A featureless office building on the adjacent corner site rises from an awkward public plaza, whilst a heritage listed two-storey sandstone 'Federation Free Style' building stands next to the proposed development. The challenge was to provide a building that mediates these odd juxtapositions of scale and type, as well as reinstating the corner junction of Quay and Thomas Streets with an expressive building that would punctuate the viewing axes along Quay and Valentine Streets.

Continuing ideas explored in the 'live' projects, particularly Coda and EDO, of the 'expressive architectural skin' – the so-called 'jacket' defining identity and character – this office tower was

north elevation

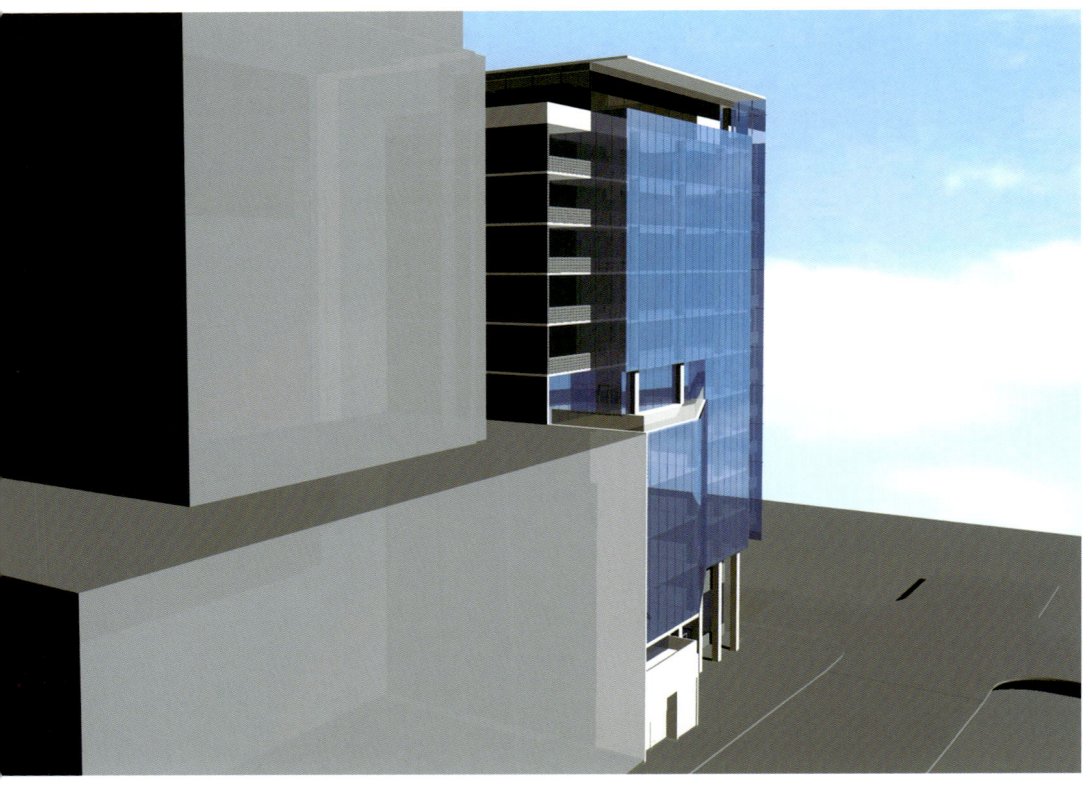

envisaged as a single form wrapped on two sides by a light, glazed surface. By contrast, the southeast and west façades then read as solid surfaces perforated with a patterned 'Klee-like' rhythm of rectangular windows. For this idea of two interlocking systems of solid and transparent, Stanisic Associates looked to the precedent of the Kaistrasse Studios in Dusseldorf by David Chipperfield Architects. The intention was that the building, when seen from the corner, would appear as a tall crystalline form rising above a solid defined base, which contains retail and the entry lobby. To establish a contextual dialogue with the scale and rhythm of adjacent buildings, a series of cuts and folds were made into the skin and building form. Particular attention was paid to the street-facing elevation adjoining the smaller two-storey heritage listed building, and to the solar access received by the apartments on the Quay Street elevation. The corner view – with a façade at once reflective and transparent, and possessing a horizontal articulation on its northwest elevation – is reminiscent of Mies van der Rohe's unbuilt Friedrichstrasse skyscraper of 1921.

In keeping with the practice's established sustainable and environmental agendas, passive solar design principles are used throughout: low-E glass is used for the glazing of the north, east and west elevations, decentralised zoned air-conditioning systems within in each office suite allow offices to be individually conditioned, and the rear light-court functions as a vertical stack for the nightly purging of heat from the office levels. Whilst the Quay project has a formal expressiveness resulting in a certain dynamism, it proposes a refined architectural identity that continues Stanisic Associates' interest in tectonic abstraction: in an urban architecture that engages with context without resorting to pastiche or overwrought architectural mannerism.

1. Retail
2. Lobby
3. Office
4. Light Court
5. Courtyard
6. Kitchen

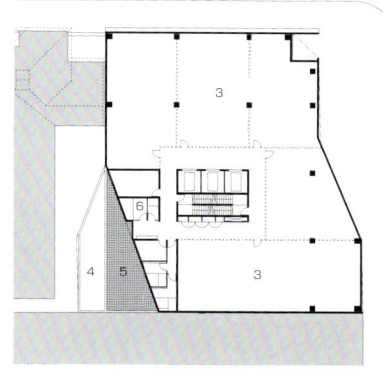

third floor and fifth floor plan

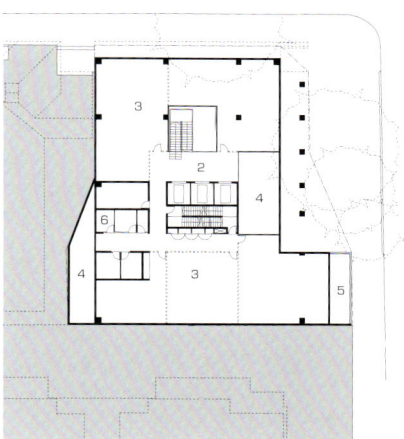

first floor plan

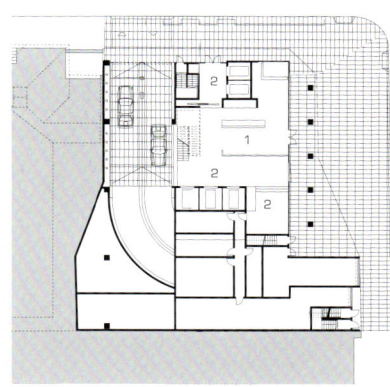

ground floor plan

Haymarket 2008 –

MISSION

One of the largest projects undertaken by Stanisic Associates, this high-rise mixed-use development, located in the inner city Haymarket area, denotes a shift in scale – to a 108-metre tower – and raises its own set of very particular design requirements. The practice's systematic and strong conceptual agendas, which underpin the architectural strategy, make for a design process that is easily transferable, as the evolution of an abstract diagrammatic architecture has, within its framework, an inherent flexibility and adaptability. Underscoring all projects is a strong agenda to address the urban context, streetscape and public amenity, and the accommodation of retail, office or apartment components is driven by a desire for passive environmental design where the architectural cues come from the development of a permeable building envelope, which is responsive to climate and place. Program does not drive expression: it is housed in an environmentally responsive architecture that takes heed of its urban context and climatic conditions. So when it came to the design of this multi-storey mixed-use development on a challenging, irregular-shaped site with narrow street frontages – bounded by high rise towers and with limited northern exposure – the approach began with the conception of the site as a malleable volume with constraints and opportunities. The architecture was then carved out and chiselled from the site, resulting in a dynamic and striking urban form, which operates across a number of programmatic levels and fulfils several site-specific roles.

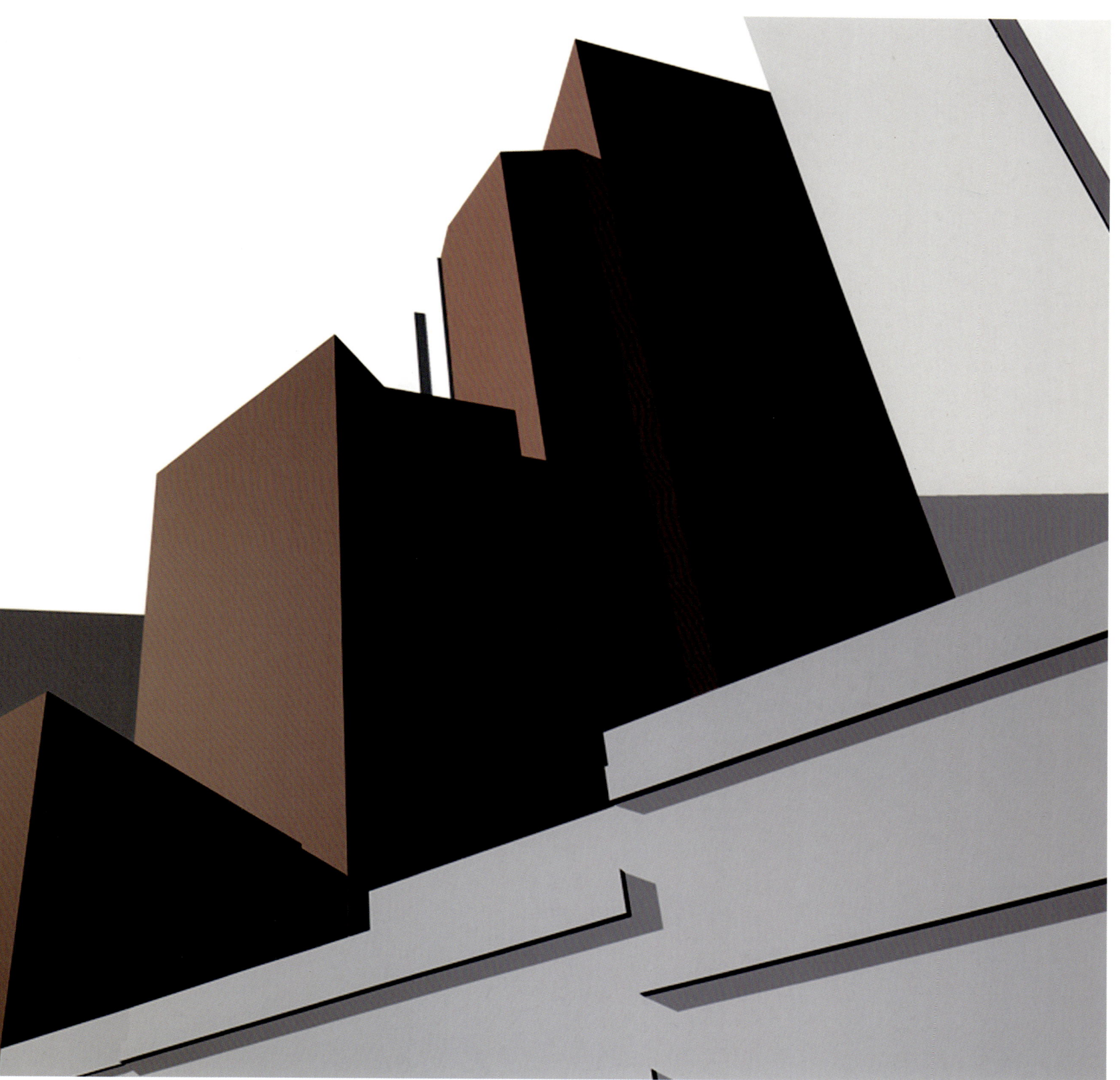

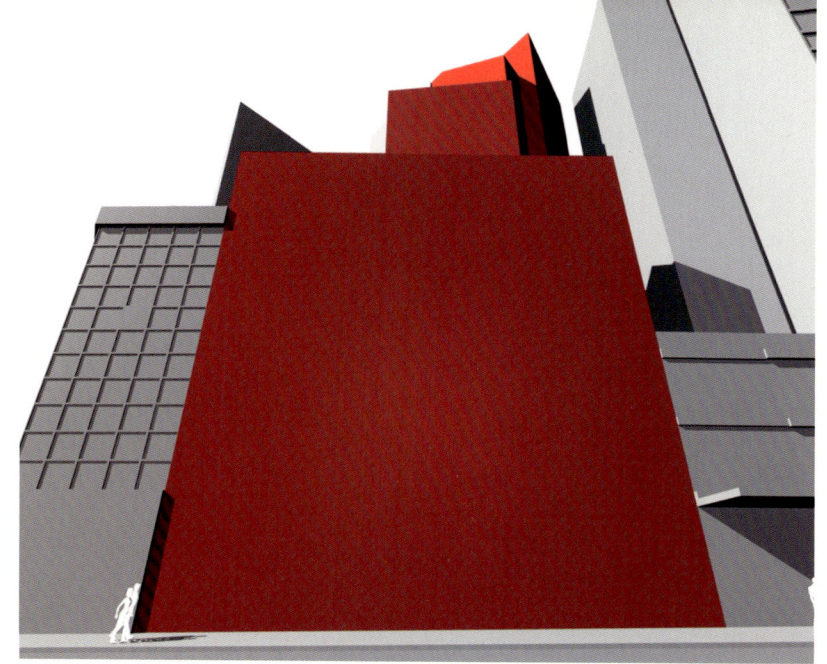

The project comprises three central interconnected building blocks layered on top of one another. A low-rise office building, with retail and recreation for the apartments, contains two paved pedestrian links: 'the high road' from Campbell Street through to Cunningham Street, and the 'low road' into the entry lobbies for the offices and serviced apartments. At ground level, the building – with its straight street-like pathways and a generous externally covered double-height forecourt with shops, a café, restaurants and a bar – operates as an urban connector, an extension of the city that ties the building back into the public pedestrian networks of its site. Seen from Campbell Street, this first element of offices – with an elevation of floor to ceiling glass shielded by a filigree of translucent glass louvre blades – has a dynamic expression that responds to the rhythms and heights of the adjacent buildings.

A twelve level mid-rise structure of serviced apartments steps back from the street as a lighter and more crystalline presence: a plane of glazed balustrades denominates the southern façade, whilst light-courts with metal cladding are employed for the southeast façade. A third high-rise tower, containing a further 17 levels of serviced apartments, is aligned to the south, and responds to the available light sources and view. Slimmer and taller than the other two blocks, and with its northeast and southwest elevations having no windows or balconies, this tower becomes a more planar and chiselled sculptural form of darkly toned precast concrete: a robust abstraction, adding a presence to the city skyline, and forming a solid backdrop for the two lighter blocks. Viewed from afar, and as fragments caught within the dense city fabric, Mission's three dimensionality – changeable and sculptural – speaks not only of Frank Stanisic's love for the work of the Constructivists and the early 20th century modernists, but also of a design sophistication, which is revealed in the overall ensemble of building elements on a very complex large-scale infill site.

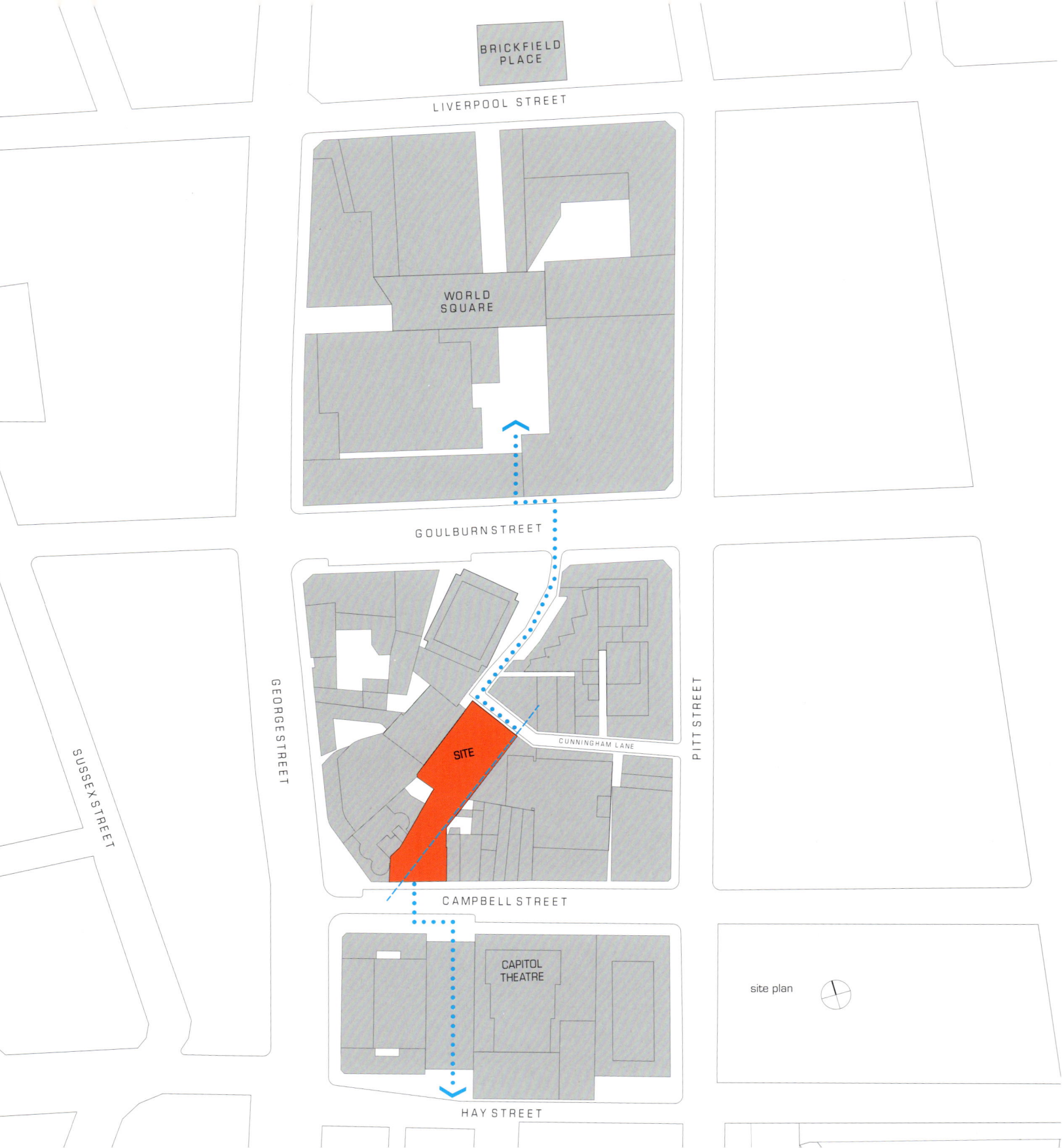

site plan

ground floor plan   0 5 10 20m

upper ground floor plan

1 Pedestrian Way
2 Forecourt
3 Café
4 Reception
5 Loading

CGIs © David Dudoy

Roseville 2008 (unbuilt)
ROSEVILLE

This striking hybrid development proposed for Roseville, in Sydney's affluent North Shore region, was an unrealised town centre demonstration project for the Ku-ring-gai Council, and one of the most comprehensive and elegant tests of Stanisic Associates' ideas to date. Operating across a diversity of urban requirements, the design – a series of five slender blocks cantilevering across a common two-storey system of courtyards and building – is a remarkably expressive and conceptually tight piece of architecture. A linear stretch of small titled lots, with a through-site pedestrian link and a mature exotic tree, is bounded by Pacific Highway to the north and Larkin Lane to the south, and forms part of an urban renewal zone adjacent to Roseville railway station and the historic Roseville Cinema. The development was required to define new public space and revive the rear laneway, whilst providing for environmentally responsive high-density living above office and retail components. The project's urban and programmatic complexities were ideally suited to the agendas of Stanisic Associates, as their explorations of a flexible, abstract architecture were able to adapt to a diversity of constraints.

A central question addressed in this project concerned the relationship of typology to the image of form. What 'image' should befit a complex integrated building that contains a variety of programs and activities? Should 'form' address that programmatic complexity, or should the image be driven by another agenda altogether? For Stanisic Associates, the expression of the building has become progressively less about the program and more about the building – the form – and how it can operate environmentally

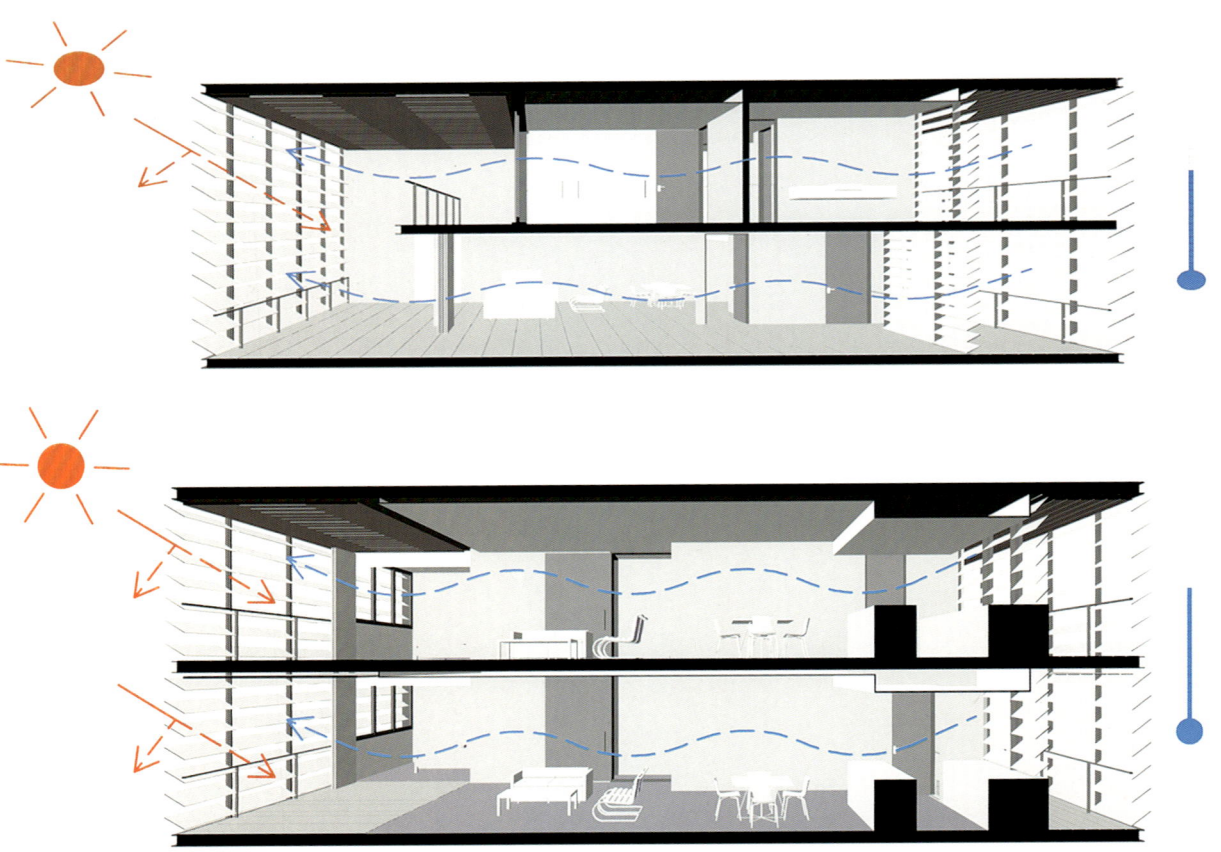

Sectional views showing solar access and cross-ventilation

and within its context. At Roseville, the form is an evolution of the environmental screen first seen in EDO and Coda. A form-wrapping filtered metal jacket is all encompassing and environmentally attuned, whilst establishing a sophisticated, refined and textured aesthetic. This strategy, as Frank Stanisic points out, avoids the arbitrary featurism and aesthetic 'free styling' common to many multi-unit housing developments. A system of fixed metal louvres and operable metal blinds allows for diverse responses to climatic conditions and an apartment's orientation. At night, and as a reference to the adjacent cinema, the building's lobbies and access galleries are animated with coloured LED lights visible through the external screen.

The five finger elements holding the apartments are organised so that they turn away from the busy highway to run parallel with the road. Giving the project an abstracted sculptural appearance, the circulation access galleries located adjacent to the road are effectively solid walls that shield the apartments from the noise. The apartments – of one, two and three bedrooms, over one and two storeys – have a dual orientation, allowing for ample natural light, cross-ventilation, and living and balcony spaces with northwest orientation. Continuing another idea from EDO, the apartments have internal sliding walls that allow a flexibility of spatial configurations. At street level, a system of fine grain connections and public spaces lead from the railway station to the existing and future housing to the west of the site. The existing public domain and pedestrian way through the site to Larkin Lane has been upgraded, and includes a protected public square around the large exotic tree. An underground car park has also been provided. The Roseville project, proposing a significant and staged strategy for urban renewal, offers a rich opportunity for high density living in close proximity to public and transportation amenities. And with its delicate striated skin, at once protecting and porous, the apartment blocks become tempered boxes: an architecture that offers an alternative language for collective housing and mixed-use projects.

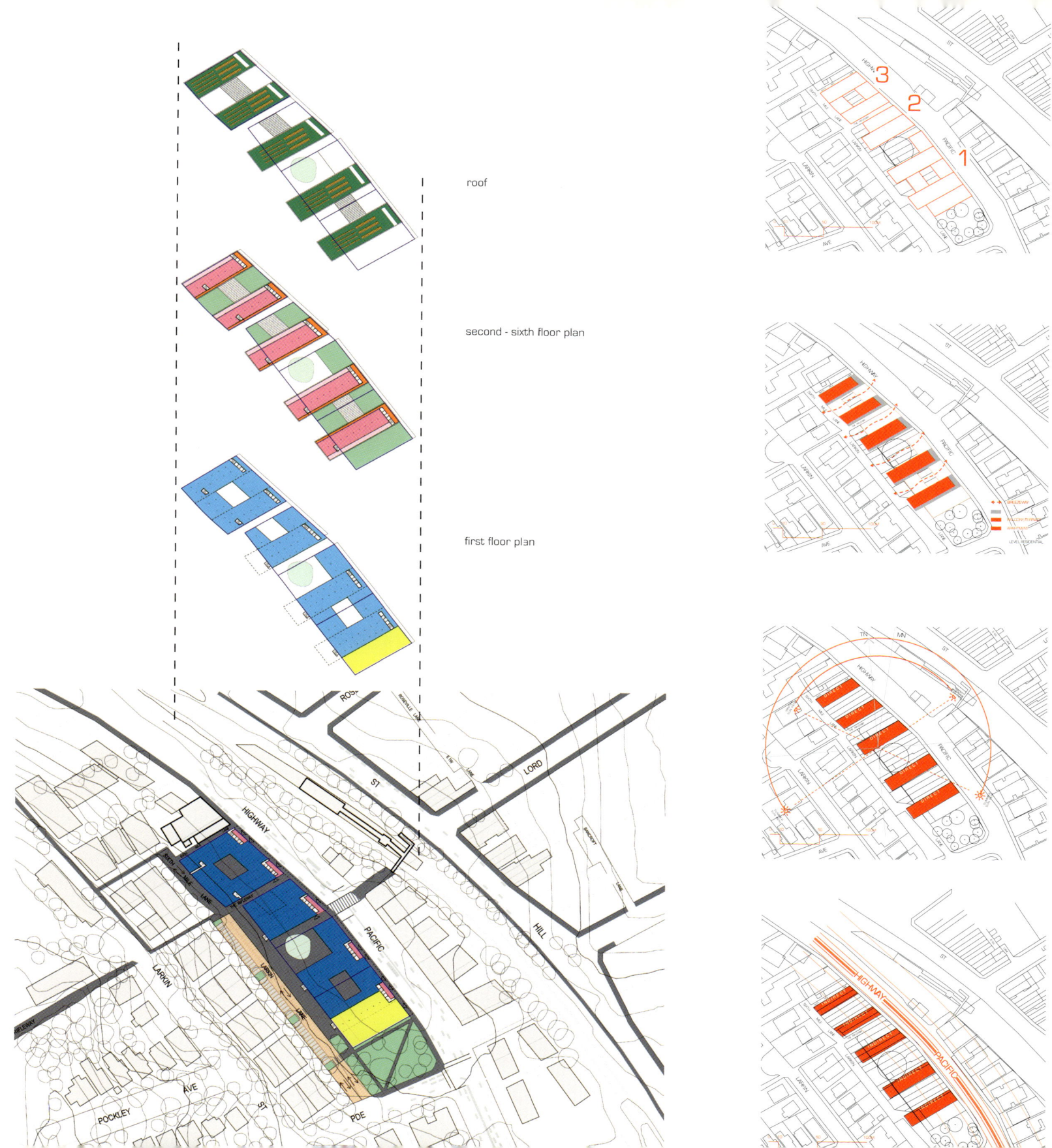

Green Square 2009 (unbuilt)

HYPERFORM

Speculative projects form a critical part of the design research process of Stanisic Associates, as realised projects do not always provide the scope or the opportunity for the intensive explorations needed to fully test ideas. For a practice that has very particular ambitions for its buildings, and their environmental, social and architectural roles, it is essential that research through design is pursued at an experimental level not constrained by site, program or finances, and Hyperform is an exciting example of this research. Over the past decade, Stanisic Associates have been exploring programmatic relationships to form, and what began as a pure investigation into environmentally-responsive collective housing has expanded to include the study of mixed use, or hybrid, types, and the consequences for architectural expression. In early projects, such as Atlas and Mondrian, program was expressed and made legible on the exterior, but this mode has become less predominant as the exterior expression has become increasingly separated from the interior, and behaves in a more performative and operable manner.

Hyperform tests these ideas through a proposal for a mixed-use development for the Green Square town centre, adjacent to the proposed Civic Plaza. Arguing that urban planners and developers should think differently about site boundaries and divisions, the architects began by redefining the site's envelope, with an explicit agenda to generate form without consideration for program: the question was how extreme could form become without regard to program? This prompted further questions as to what drives form and, critically, what happens when a hybrid program of 'live', 'work' and 'shop', is pushed into that formal framework. Hyperform is an

exploration of form and type where, as Frank Stanisic argues, the result is a transformation of type. Hyperform moves beyond mixed-use into the evolution of another single type, which began with the transformation of the gallery access circulation system. Typically the design process of the practice begins with a box – a slim-line perimeter edge – with a gallery system at the back, but Hyperform begins with a massive solid block into which voids have been cut in and out: the box is magnified, the perimeter edge is folded into the block, and circulation systems are woven through the centre. The streetscape is extended through the building, and attaches itself to the network of through-site links, circulation, and private and communal courtyards.

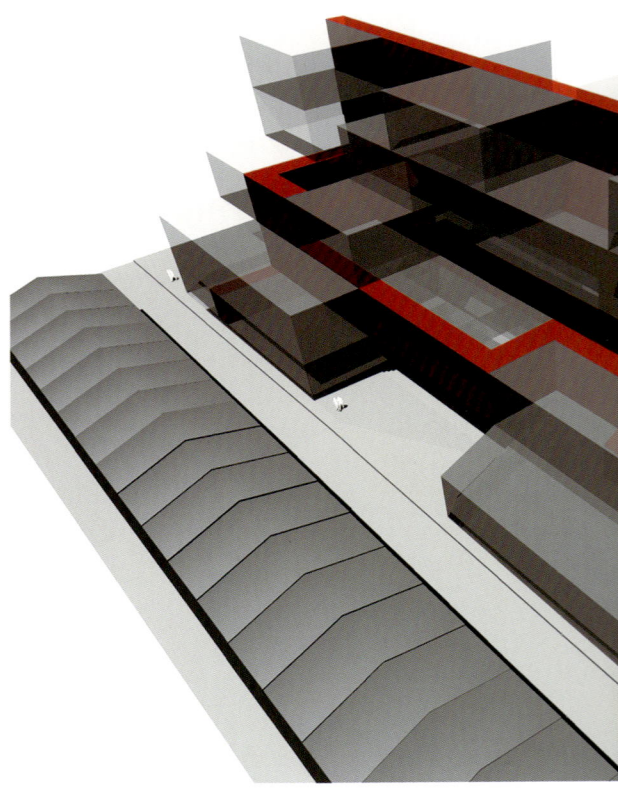

This system of voids, deep recesses, platforms and green roofs, with the program 'pushed' into the mass, transforms the project into a honeycomb structure. The first two levels accommodate cultural civic activity – shops, cinemas and offices – whilst the upper eight storeys comprise living areas, open public spaces and roof gardens. These external spaces test alternative ways to live and use open spaces when the occupation and program is hybrid and, as already explored in EDO and Coda, the exterior form is 'skinned' with an environmental envelope made up of a uniform 'jacket' of shutters and louvres. Hyperform operates as a critique of the unsustainable low-density suburb – with detached dwellings, front fences and driveways – and offers an alternative: a massive urban-scaled block providing density, diversity and individuality. The project was an attempt to think laterally about site and form, and the evolution of a non-prescriptive model for living.

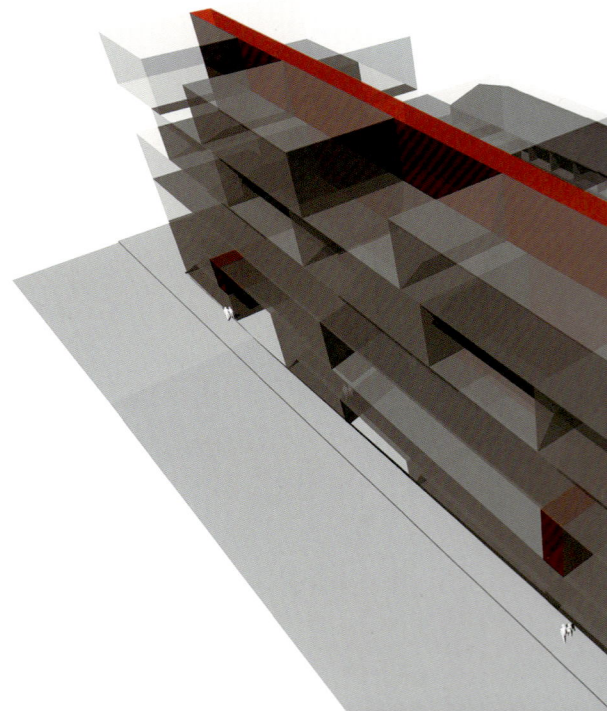

Hyperform

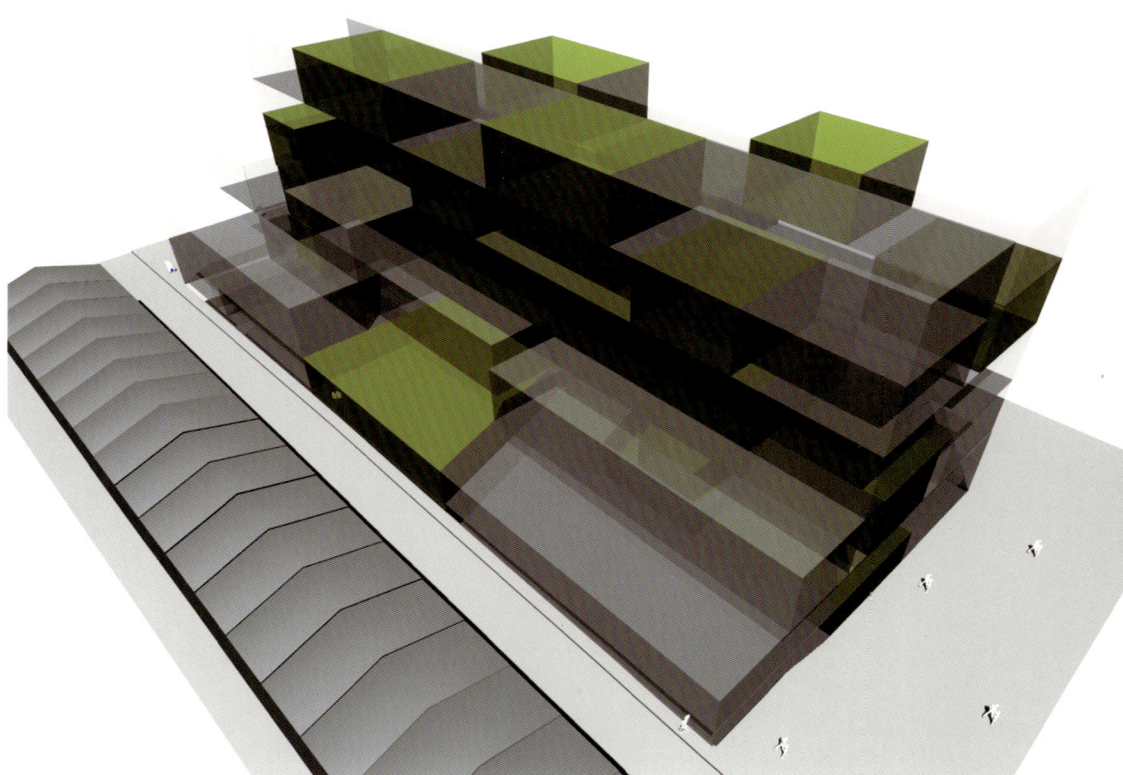
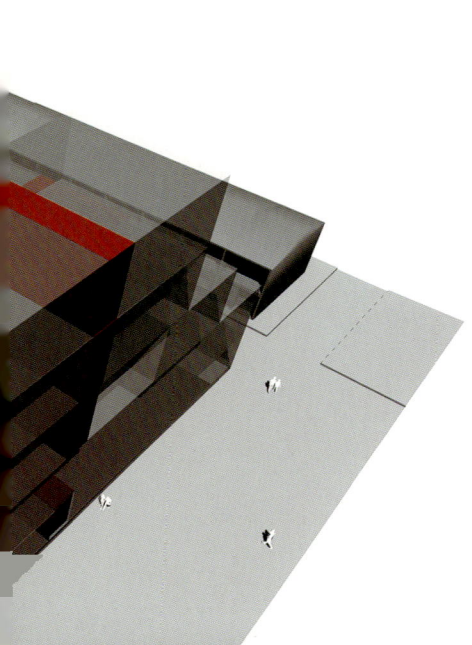
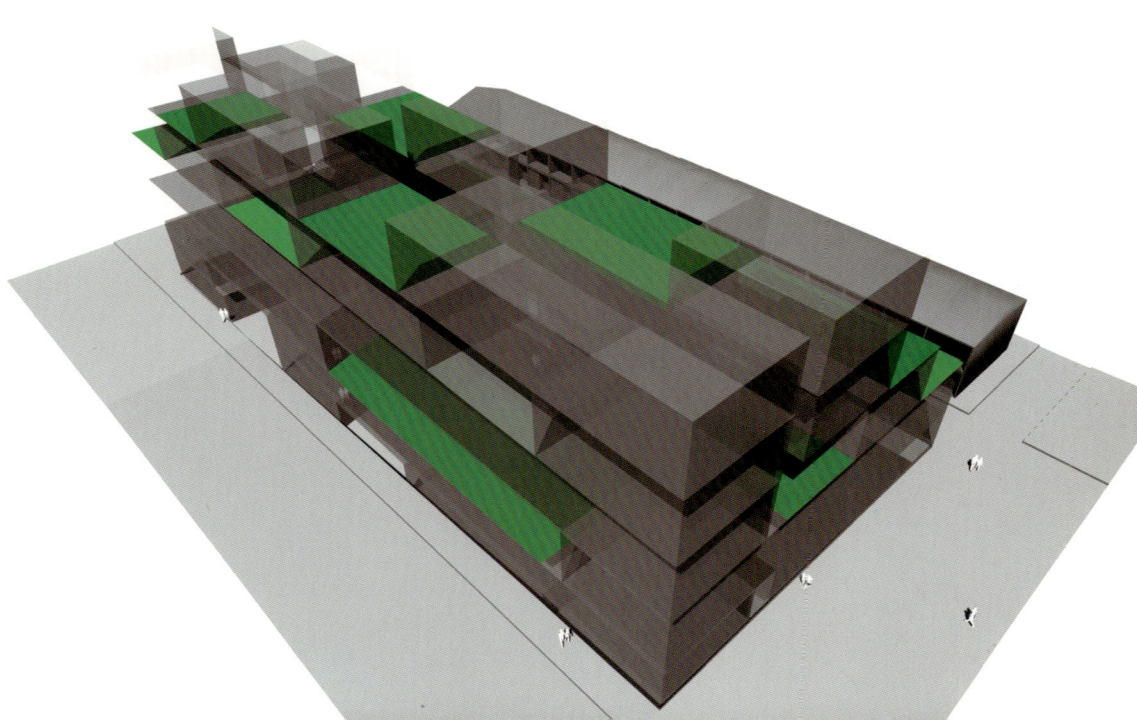

Hyperform

stanisic LIVE/WORK 2000-2010

stanisic associates team members

Adam Hobbs . Adam Russell . Adrian Curtin . Alain Assoum . Aleks Jelicic . Alfonso Casanova . Aline Hoechstetter . Andrew Buchanan . Andrew Donnelly . Angela Rheinlaender . Angelo Roumeliotis . Anke Ramin . Belinda Edmonds . Ben Giles . Carsten Hilgendorf . Cathal O'Boyle . Christian Bruna . Christopher Hewson . Christopher Solek . Claire Grigg . Damien Madell . David Cook . David Tickle . Dinah Zhang . Dita Logar . Doug Hamilton . Emmet Rogan . Francis Falzon . Frank Stanisic . Franka Boehm . George Argioropoulos . Glen Wong . Greg Williams . Hanny Liem . Isaac Franzini . Ivan Ip . Ines Klein . Jason Nowosad . Joanna Wing Yan Ng . John Bralic . Jose Serrao . Juan Manzano . Karen Whiteley . Katharine Young . Kate O'Brien . Kenneth Ho . Laurence Cheung . Martin Hagemann . Martin Stanisic Logar . Michael Wells . Mike Harris . Mitsuru Delisle . Monique Knifka . Moritz Rinne . Peter Rush . Quetzal Diaz de Leon . Renn Holland . Richard Chan . Rob Harper . Rod Pindar . Roland Hinz . Runyuan Xu . Silvana Chocano . Stephan Gutman . Stefan Meissner . Sue Liew . Summant Tanna . Teresa Vrbova . Terence Weng Shun Yong . Tobias Kunst . Uwe Stache . Yi-der Ho

landscape architects   Aspect Sydney . McGregor Partners . McGregor Coxall . Oculus . John Locke

environmental engineers   Cundall

structural engineers   TTW . Partridge Partners . SCP Consulting . BG+E Consulting Engineers . Robert Bird Group . Low and Hook

planning   JBA Urban Planning . BBC Consulting Partners

services engineers   ITC Services . George Floth Services . Michael Frost and Associates . Warren Smith and Partners

clients   Tuglow . Walters Developments . St Hilliers Developments . Newtown Developments . Lupure . Epson Developments GMD and GHD . Calwood Developments . Walker Group . Mirvac . Lateral Corporation . Buildcorp Property Developments . Hayson Group . Amitran . Stockland . Bernleigh Developments . Meriton . Karimbla Constructions

special thanks for support on the book

Dinah Zhang . Runyuan Xu . Martin Stanisic Logar . Dita Logar . Peter John Cantrill

essay and all project descriptions © Anna Johnson

additional essays © Philip Drew . Tom Heneghan . Tarsha Finney

all photography © Patrick Bingham-Hall, except where otherwise credited

awards

2011   AIA Architecture Award . Commercial . **Era**
         AIA Architecture Award . Finalist . Sustainability . **Era**
         AIA Architecture Award . Finalist . Urban Design . **Era**

2010   BPN/Environ Sustainability Award . Small Commercial . **Era**
         AIA Architecture Award . Finalist . Multiple Housing . **Coda**

2009   AIA Architecture Award . Finalist . Multiple Housing . **Coda**

2008   AIA Frederick Romberg Award . Multiple Housing . **EDO**
         AIA Aaron Bolot Award . Multiple Housing . **EDO**
         BPN/Environ Sustainability Award . Commendation . High Density Housing . **Coda**

2007   BPN/Environ Sustainability Award . Low Density Housing . **EDO**
         RAIA Architecture Award . Finalist . Residential . **EDO**

2006   RAIA Special Jury Award . **Zone** and **Spectrum**

2004   UDIA Mixed Use Project Award . **Rhodes Waterside, Lot 4**
         FGS/TAS Gold Medal . Green Building Award . **Mondrian**
         FGS/TAS Silver Medal . Green Building Award . **Spectrum**

2003   RAIA Wilkinson Award . Residential . **Mondrian**
         MBA Excellence in Housing Award . **Mondrian**

2002   RAIA Civic Design . Finalist . **Spanish Quarter**
         RAIA Architecture Award . Finalist . Residential . **Presidio**
         RAIA Architecture Award . Finalist . Residential . **Atlas**
         SSDC Green Square Design Award . **Eco**
         SSDC Green Square Design Commendation . **Mondrian**
         Green City Residential Award, Hurstville City Council . **Forest Ridge**
         Marrickville Medal Commendation, Marrickville Council . **Domain**

2001   RAIA Premier's Award for Excellence in Residential Design . **Domain**

special thanks for contributions to projects

Angela Rheinlaender . Adam Russell . Ben Giles . Christian Bruna . Damien Madell . Jason Nowosad . Rob Harper . Stefan Meissner

Copyright for Domain, Presidio and Atlas is © Stanisic Turner Architects